AFTER

Kristya,
Thank you for
your support!
Happy Rea[ding]
♡ RJ Belle

R.J. BELLE

AFTER

THE BATTLE HAS JUST BEGUN

www.AuthorRJBelle.com
AuthorRJBelle@yahoo.com

Grateful acknowledgement is made to Stuart Witt for permission to reprint "Final Flight" and Laura Landaker for sharing her letter and memories of her son with us.

Edited by Helen Gerth Mahi
Cover Design by Kiran Kumar Banala, creative designer, India
Interior Layout by Maureen Cutajar
Book Trailer by LoewenHerz-Creative
With original music by Greg White Jr.

First publication March 2016

ISBN-10: 0-9966235-1-5
ISBN-13: 978-0-9966235-1-3

For those who gave everything.

Editor's note: Final Flight (Chapter 1 opening) was written by Stuart Witt of Ridgecrest, Manager at Mojave Airport, Bakersfield, CA and former US Navy F-14/F-18 pilot, on the final flight of 1st Lt Jared Landaker, USMC, who was killed in Iraq on February 07, 2007. He was aboard the flight from Washington, D. C. to Los Angeles February 17, 2007 with the Landaker family as they brought their son home for burial. I felt it important enough to run it in its entirety exactly as it was written.

Author's note: Interviews conducted for the purpose of writing this book were recorded. In all areas where a direct quote is given, I have listened to the audio taped interview to assure quoted accuracy. Any inaccuracy of reported information in the recounting of stories from the battlefield or elsewhere by those I interviewed is not intentional. All possible measures were taken to insure accuracy of information. Some names have been removed, shortened or changed out of courtesy to all parties involved.

Some of the stories in this book contain erratic shifts in verb tense. These are left in deliberately to allow the reader to hear the stories from the veteran's perspective. The violence and trauma of many stories included in this book are still vivid and painful.

CONTENTS

AFTER

The Battle Has Just Begun

"Out of every one hundred men, ten shouldn't even be there, eighty are just targets, nine are the real fighters, and we are lucky to have them, for they make the battle. Ah, but the one, one is a warrior, and he will bring the others back."

—HERACLITUS

CHAPTER 1

FINAL FLIGHT

By Stuart Witt

———»«O»«———

Feb. 17, 2007, 0350 curbside at 24th and M, Washington DC. 16 degrees with a light breeze. Going home after my second week of freezing temps. Fly my aircraft, ride a horse, climb a mountain and get back to living. I'm tired of the cold.

0425 paying the taxi fare at Dulles in front of the United Airlines counter, still cold.

0450 engaging the self-serve ticker machine and it delivers my ticket, baggage tag and boarding pass. Hmmm, that Marine is all dressed up early...? Oh, maybe... Hmmm, "Good morning captain, you're looking sharp."

Pass security and to my gate for a quick decaf coffee and five hours sleep. A quick check of the flight status monitor and UA Flight 211 is on time. I'm up front, how bad can it be? Hmmm, that same Marine, he must be heading to Pendleton to see his lady at LAX for the long weekend all dressed up like that....? Or maybe not?

"Attention in the boarding area, we will begin boarding in 10 minutes, we have some additional duties to attend to this morning but we will have you out of here on time."

1

That captain now has five others with him. BINGO. I get it, he is not visiting his lady, he's an official escort. How I remember doing that once, CACO duty. I still remember the names of the victim and family, The Bruno family in Mojave ..., all of them, wow, that was 24 years ago. I wonder if we will ever know who and why?

On board, 0600: "Good morning folks this is the captain. This morning we have been attending to some additional duties and I apologize for being 10 minutes late for pushback but believe me we will be early to LAX. This morning it is my sad pleasure to announce that 1st Lt. Jared Landaker, USMC, will be flying with us to his Big Bear home in Southern California.

"Jared lost his life over the skies of Iraq earlier this month and today we have the honor of returning him home along with his mother, father, brother and uncles. Please join me in making the journey comfortable for the Landaker family and their uniformed escort. Now sit back and enjoy our ride, we are not expecting any turbulence until we reach the

Rocky Mountains and at that time we will do what we can to ensure a smooth ride. For those interested you can listen in to our progress on button 9."

Up button 9: "Good morning UA 211 you are cleared to taxi, takeoff and cleared to LAX as filed." From the time we started rolling we never stopped. 1st Lt. Landaker began receiving his due.

Four hours and 35 minutes later, over Big Bear Mountain, the AB320 makes a left roll and steep bank and then one to the right, Nice touch captain

"Five minutes out from landing, the captain: "Ladies and gents, after landing I'm leaving the fasten seatbelt sign on and I ask everyone in advance to yield to the Landaker family. Please remain seated until all members have departed the aircraft. Thank you for your patience, we are 20 minutes early."

On roll out, I notice red lights, emergency vehicles everywhere. We are being escorted directly to our gate, no waiting anywhere, not even a pause. Out the left window, a dozen Marines in full dress blues. Highway Patrol, police, fire crews all in full dress with lights on. A true class act by everyone, down to a person, from coast to coast. Way to go United Airlines for doing the little things RIGHT, because they are the big things; Air Traffic Control for getting the message, to all law enforcement for your display of brotherhood.

When the family departed the aircraft everyone sat silent, then I heard a lady say, "God Bless You and your Family, Thank You." Then another, then another, then a somber round of applause. The captain read a prepared note from Mrs. Landaker to the effect, "Thank you all for your patience and heartfelt concern for us and our son. We sincerely appreciate the sentiment. It is nice to have Jared home."

After departing the aircraft, I found myself, along with 30 others from our flight, looking for a window. Not a dry eye in the craft. All of us were bawling like babies. It was one of the most emotional moments of my life. We all stood silent and watched as Jared was taken by his honor guard to an awaiting hearse. Then the motorcade slowly made its way off the ramp.

I have finally seen the silent majority. It is deep within us all. Black, Brown, White, Yellow, Red, Purple, we are all children, parents, brothers, sisters, etc ... we are an American family.

What you don't know is that on the flight I was tapped on the shoulder by Mrs. Landaker who introduced herself to me after I awoke. Her words were, "I understand you have sons in the service. Please tell them we appreciate their service. We are so proud of our kids who chose to serve at this time. We were so proud of Jared and today we find ourselves in a fog of disbelief. Jared was three days from returning home."

Early in our taxi out from the gate at Dulles, the gent next to me (a Fairfax City Council Member and acquaintance of the Thuot family) and I were talking to the flight attendant and mentioned that we had sons serving on active duty, "What do you say? How tragic, they must be devastated." He said many of the passengers had told him the same thing so somewhere in the flight he shared his tidbits with Mrs. Landaker. Our flight attendant had been struggling with what to say, to find the right words, so he told the Landaker family of passengers who were parents of service members who connected with their grief as parents. After I gathered myself, I stepped back to their row, two behind me and introduced myself to Mr. Landaker (a Veteran of South East Asia as a Tanker) and Jared's uncle and brother. What a somber moment. Their Marine captain escort was a first rate class act. He had been Jared's tactics instructor and volunteered for this assignment, as he said, "Sir, it is the least I could do, he was my friend and a great stick. He absolutely loved to fly, It's an honor to be here on his last flight."

1115: On my connecting flight, my mind raced. How lucky I was to have had an opportunity to fly my father to Spain and ride the carrier USS John F. Kennedy home in 1981. The same year Jared was born. How lucky I was to have my father on the crows landing when I made my final cat shot in an F-14. Jared's father never had that chance. Jared was at war, 10,000 miles away.

When Mr. Landaker and I were talking he shared with me, "When Jared was born he had no soft spot on his head and doctors feared he would be developmentally challenged. He became a physics major with honors, a high school and college athlete, and graduated with distinction from naval aviation flight school. He was short in stature, but a Marine all the way." Visit his life story on line at www.BigBearGrizzly.net. Bring tissue.

February 7, 2007, Anbar Province, Iraq. 1st Lt Jared Landaker, United States Marine Corps, Hero, from Big Bear Calif., gave his life in service to his country. Fatally wounded when his CH-46 helicopter was shot down by enemy fire, Jared and his crew all perished. His life was the ultimate sacrifice of a grateful military family and nation.

His death occurred at the same time as Anna Nicole Smith, a drug using person with a 7th grade education of no pedigree who dominated our news for two weeks while Jared became a number on CNN. And most unfortunately, Jared's death underscores a fact that we are a military at war, not a nation at war. Until we become a nation committed to winning the fight, and elect leaders with the spine to ask Americans to sacrifice in order to win, we shall remain committed to being a nation with a military at war, and nothing more. (And possibly no funding if congress has their way!)

1st Lt. Landaker, a man I came to know in the skies over America on 17 February 2007, from me to you, aviator to aviator, I am unbelievably humbled. It was my high honor to share your last flight. God bless you. Semper Fi.

———•———

I have been contemplating on how to put into words what my life has been like since the loss of Jared. What comes to mind are the constant states of loss and survival; coping with the loss of the child, the loss of your identity as their mother, and the loss of knowing how to move forward. The survival state begins at the same time you begin dealing with the realization of your loss. Can I survive my child's death; the constant heartache you carry with you daily; will your marriage survive the loss; will our family ever feel peace again; and will we ever find joy and be able to smile when thinking of your loved one?

When I became a mother my life changed for the better in so many ways. I believe I actually knew when I conceived Jared even though it would not be confirmed for several weeks. His birth was unique for Joe and me as I gave birth to him at home with Joe delivering him. But on February 7, 2007, with the sound of multiple footsteps and three knocks on our door, life would change again for me, but not for the better. A month prior to this date, a CH-46 had gone down in the Al Anbar Province where Jared was stationed. I emailed him to make sure he was alright. A few hours passed before he responded with a short "I am fine".

But on February 7, 2007, it was a different response. A scroll across the bottom of the TV screen saying a CH-46 had gone down in the same area. I ran to the computer and wrote to Jared to make sure it wasn't him. There was not too much information on the incident as Anna Nicole Smith had passed that day and she took over the news. By noon there still was no response and somewhere deep inside I knew he would not be coming home. Jared was supposed to come home earlier than his Squadron to attend a Weapons and Tactics course in

Yuma, AZ, to become an Instructor. Jared had finished his regular flights at that time and was preparing to return stateside. I recounted his flights and felt sure he was not one of the pilots, only to learn later he had been picked to fly with Capt. Jennifer Harris on her last flight before returning to teach at a local college back home.

As I waited to hear any news, I thought if I would just hang out in town they could not find me and inform me my son had been killed. As it turned out they did find me and the nightmare began. I had just returned from town and was walking down the hall when I heard the footsteps and knocks. I turned to see two Marines and a Navy Chaplain all in uniform waiting for me to open the door. I hollered to my husband that they were here. He asked who and I just said, "the Marines"! He collapsed on the floor crying and just kept saying, "he was supposed to come home next week"! Our lives were changed forever in that instant. It is interesting how your mind helps you survive the loss of this magnitude. I remember bits and pieces of what followed: bringing Jared home from Dover; following the Hearst down the hill; the ceremony and flag presentation; and finally, watching him descend into the earth.

The loss of Jared has changed the dynamics of our family in so many ways. There is only the past left when I think of my son, no present, no future. His memory is frozen in my mind and a constant worry I am going to forget them. There is a sadness that flows over me at times. It is not sadness for myself, for I had the pleasure of being his mom for 25 years. My sadness is for him and all that he will never experience. He will never fall in love, watch her walk down the aisle to become his partner; never see and touch his newborn child for the first time; and so much more. There is always a persistent wondering of what he would look like today, would he be married, would he have children, etc. All the firsts dates of a child's life that are so special to a parent are now dreaded ones. His birthday and the anniversary of his death are the most difficult. One gave him life and one took his life. On his birthday I no longer throw a party and give him a card telling him how much I love him. Now I go to his resting place and post on his Legacy board.

May 6, 2014

Dear Jare: on your 33rd birthday I spent it honoring you and a WW2 Vet in Washington, DC. I escorted the Vet to the WW2 Memorial, a place he never thought he would ever get to see in his lifetime. I listened to his stories of war and life afterward and I shared your life as well. There was a common bond between the both of you that made me so proud of you two and the sacrifices made for our freedoms. Love and miss you more every day, but especially on your birthday.

Mom

Through Jared's loss I have gained an inner strength I never expected or knew I had. There is a survival instinct deep inside that forces me to get up each day and to look for the joy and peace living offers. I know that is Jared.

—Laura Landaker

CHAPTER 2

A DIFFERENT TYPE OF AFTER

———— ≈《●》≈ ————

This project was born from a desire to heighten awareness about the need for services that cater to combat injured service members; specifically the need for services that assist in the transition from military to civilian life after a service related injury.

Working with Warrior Foundation ~ Freedom Station was eye-opening from day one, so much so that I made the decision to write a book about this amazing organization that very day. What has transpired between the day I made that decision and now has been one of the most difficult journeys I have ever attempted to write about. I am still unsure if I can adequately articulate the magnitude of loss, strength, sacrifice, inspiration, and 'wow' moments that I have experienced and been able to document in the process of the interviews I conducted.

Early on in the process of crafting the foundation for this project, I requested to interview a few of the men who resided at Freedom Station. I never imagined that it would become so all-consuming, emotionally draining or magnificently inspiring. The interview process was akin to giving pieces of my well-guarded soul away, slowly and in the most heartbreaking ways possible. It was also an awakening I've never before experienced. I have learned about strength and courage and, most importantly, sacrifice. Real sacrifice. I have learned what it means to give and to struggle. I have learned what feeling helpless looks like and I have learned what picking one's self up actually takes. It takes a lot. By a lot I mean it takes an absolute, iron will and a deeply rooted desire to move forward. It takes the stuff that most of us aren't made of. I am lost when I try to come up with an adjective or paint a picture with words of what it takes. Through this book, these stories and the statistics I uncovered along the way – I hope to paint an accurate and truthful picture of what *AFTER* looks and feels like for the men and women who survived as well as what *AFTER* is like for the loved ones of those who didn't.

There are two types of *AFTER*.

There is the after that the families of the fallen live each and every day. I felt that the opening of this book should begin with a story of such an after. I believe every person that I interviewed would agree that it is the fallen and those who mourn them that, at least partially, fuels their drive to move forward and build lives worthy of honoring the ones who did not return home alive.

There is another type of after and that type of after is often lost in the rush to move back to 'normalcy', the need to somehow put the horror of war behind. This book is for them. This book is for those who assist them. This book is the story of going on after war. But make no mistake – the war will never be over for these men and women. For them, the battle has just begun.

CHAPTER 3

THE STATISTICS

———— ((O)) ————

Statistics provide us with data, and data can build solid infrastruc-
tures and lay foundations. It can help us 'see', but it can't help us
feel the reality of a lived experience. It can't replace the personal stories that breathe life into the statistics.

I have spent a considerable amount of time researching statistics
both on national and local levels. Before we go over some of the data
I have uncovered, I want to make it clear what this book is about and,
more importantly, what it is not about.

This book is not about politics. It isn't about presidents or parties.
It wasn't written to push right or left wing agendas or to justify the
actions or inactions of any political party. This book is not about being pro or anti war, the right to or not to bear arms, oil, or any other
issue that I see constantly raised, torn apart, built up and splashed all
over the front pages of media outlets to support specific agendas. The
front pages have been littered with conflicting 'data' and interpreta-
tions for so long that often Americans no longer understand or
remember why we ended up over there and, of course, that statement
in and of itself is usually cause for debate.

There was a time when I too was quick to pick up the sword of words and throw down my best argument for the why's of war, specifically this war. But that all changed when I was given a unique position to study the aftermath first hand. My perception changed, drastically. I came to understand that there is a much bigger picture, a human picture that is more often than not lost on those of us who were not directly affected by the human tragedies of war. Our most important resource, those who volunteer to serve in our military, should be our first and biggest priority. Those that come home wounded should never have to wonder or worry about how they are going to put the pieces back together – they should not be alone in that process.

The number of service members killed in action from 2001 through July 2015 is staggering at first glance. These numbers should be shocking to anyone viewing them. It is important to note that they pale in comparison to those of the Vietnam era. I only mention that because I believe it is important to recognize the gravity of loss that era suffered. Our veterans from the Vietnam era sustained immeasurable loss and injury. Instead of coming home to support and services to assist them in dealing with life after war, they returned home and faced another enemy. A new enemy. An enemy that I presume they didn't expect. They came home to an appalling display of disrespect and hatred. By us; the American people. We failed them then – we continue to do so today.

The improved services that our post 9/11 veterans have available to them is, in my opinion, a direct result of what the Vietnam veterans faced when they returned home. Many of that era banded together forming groups and organizations to establish protocol that would ensure no future warriors would suffer the same upon coming home from war.

The Congressional Research Service includes statistics published by the Department of Defense and cites the following statistics for our post 9/11 service members:

Killed in action total through 6-2015:
6,855

Wounded in action:
52,351

Deployed service members clinically diagnosed with Post Traumatic Stress Disorder (PTSD):
138,197

Traumatic Brain Injury (TBI) diagnosed for deployed and non-deployed service members:
327,299

Major limb amputations:
1,645

Let those numbers sink in for a moment.

Think about this – *wounded in action* only accounts for those who have physical injures from battle. That number does not include those who saw the injuries take place. That number doesn't include the corpsmen that worked on the broken bodies or the flight medics who did their best to keep those men and women breathing during transport to a hospital facility. It doesn't include the pilots who extracted the broken bodies and transported them to safety, and it doesn't include any of the men and women who watched their fellow service members die on the battleground.

What's left when those who are broken physically and mentally return home is a statistic that nobody can equate to numbers or percentages. What's left *after* is an unknown and often untold trauma that shouldn't be overlooked and it shouldn't go uncounted; it matters.

We have a huge percentage of our population thus adversely affected by war and to pretend like it isn't an issue is naive, at best. It affects everything: our families, our workplaces, our voting tendencies and our economy.

Our future generations – the small children living in households where dads and moms return, broken – being a part of that will shape the way they think, the way they act, trust, love. It will affect everything they do. And, without services that actually help those moms and dads to move forward in a positive direction, the long-term outcome will change all of us. To believe that the war is over and that we can all go back to business as usual – to the way it was before 9/11 – is a dangerous place for our nation to be.

Can we fix it? I don't know. I don't believe we can fix it completely. It's a bell that can't be unwrung. It happened and there is no going back. However, I strongly believe that we can help. We can make the road easier with meaningful assistance and services in place. But those services must remain in place for the duration. Our troops that come back injured aren't going to be cured in a month, a year or ten years. Their recovery will take a lifetime. The rest of their days will be spent trying to re-establish some sense of normalcy. For those that return with missing limbs and brain injuries – there is not even the appearance of 'normal'. They face a lifetime of learning to adapt. For the ones who return with emotional and psychological scars while they may achieve the appearance of 'normal' – they too will spend a lifetime learning to adapt. There is no magic pill that will make them forget.

This book is about what the *AFTER* can look like with adequate support for our wounded service members.

It is about the *AFTER* for a handful of our wounded and the reemergence of lives torn apart by war and the Foundation that has assisted in that process for so many.

CHAPTER 4

DEFINING A HERO

A hero according to Merriam-Webster is a mythological or legendary figure often of divine descent endowed with great strength or ability; an illustrious warrior; a man admired for his achievements and noble qualities; one who shows great courage.

I began pondering this word, this title when I started tracking the answers given to me by the men interviewed for this book. I asked each of them to tell me their definition of a hero. The answers I received were surprisingly similar until I came to one man. His answer was quite different, and it got me thinking – and doing research.

The word hero is of Latin origin with the first known usage in the 14th century. I submit that our modern day usage of the word is far different than was initially intended. The frequency with which our society bestows the label of hero on someone is careless, bordering on reckless.

Doing an internet search for heroes will bring results from sports stars to Superman and just about anything in between. I'm not sure how being born with a natural athleticism makes one worthy of being labeled a hero. I read story after story of people given the title of hero and found numerous articles that made me scratch my head and contemplate what the author thought when they drafted the article. I understood what the man mentioned above was trying to articulate when giving me his answer. Part of his answer included the statement, "I am offended, honestly, when someone calls me a hero. I don't want to be put in the same category as some basketball player. What I did, what I survived and what a ball player does are not the same."

I must agree.

The other answers I received upon asking the question were all similar to each other. Each man that I asked this question of replied that they do not consider themselves heroes. They feel that title belongs exclusively to those who gave their lives on the battlefield. Although I agree that those who paid the ultimate price are deserving of the title of a hero; I also believe each man interviewed in this book is just as deserving.

Being injured in combat is not what makes these men heroes. What they have done since their injuries is what earns them that title. They have each continued the fight. They have each battled their demons and pushed through excruciating surgeries, physical therapy, and learned how to adapt and thrive in their new lives. They continue the battle on a daily basis often overcome with the desire to give up, but they push on ever moving forward and providing inspiration for others out there who feel they can't go on. They set the example of what's possible with adequate support and the motivation to continue building a solid foundation on which to excel in their chosen directions. They remind us all that anything is possible and that loss is often a gateway to creating a bigger future than they ever dreamed possible. Many of them discovered a calling to serve others just as they did when they entered the military. Their service did not end when they were injured. They continue to perform acts of service providing hope and encouragement to anyone who is lucky enough to cross their paths.

It is this message of hope in the face of adversity, of service as a means of healing and honoring those who have fallen that I hope readers will hear as they read these men's stories of 'after' and consider the next time they are moved to use the term 'hero'.

CHAPTER 5

DEFINING THE NEED

———————

Many people question why there is still a need for non-profits that benefit injured military members. With the media consistently announcing the wind-down of the war, we are apt to believe that the needs are winding down as well. Some areas don't require the amount of support that has been given at the height of the war, but numerous areas suffer greatly when donation dollars dry up.

Looking at post 9/11 statistics alone brings to light the fact that our injured continue to have a need for services. With 52,351 wounded in action; 1,645 with major limb amputations and over 400,000 suffering with Traumatic Brian Injuries and Post Traumatic Stress Disorders it is obvious that there is a great need. Without proper support in place, the eventual outcome for many of our returning wounded service members will be chronic homelessness, substance abuse, and even suicide in too many cases.

As reported by the 2014 Annual Assessment Report to Congress on Veteran Homelessness, more than 1 in 10 homeless adults are veterans and California had the highest number of veterans experiencing homelessness – almost a quarter of the national homeless veteran population or 24%. There are 22.5 million veterans in the US and between

549,000 – 840,000 veterans are homeless at some point in a year. On any given night more than 300,000 veterans are living on the streets or in shelters. Veterans are twice as likely as other Americans to face chronic homelessness and the number of Vietnam era homeless veterans is greater than the number of service members killed in that war.

Lack of income due to limited education and transferable skills, combat-related injuries and illnesses, mental health issues, substance abuse, weak social networks due to difficulty adjusting to civilian life and lack of services are the primary causes for the staggering number of homeless veterans.

Vietnam era veterans suffered intolerable conditions, lack of services and a negative American sentiment upon returning home. Many of them joined together to put measures in place that would protect future generations from facing the same fate upon returning from war. It is true that we have come a long way in caring for our returning combat-injured service members, but there is still much work to be done. One of the worst things we can do is to cut services because we think the war is over. For our injured service members, the war will never be over.

Although I do not believe that viewing this issue in dollars should be the priority, I do understand those that feel the financial impact should be the deciding factor in providing services. I submit that the economic impact of growing homelessness and joblessness will create a larger financial burden than providing proactive services that continue through an injured service member's lifetime. I also submit that the economic impact should never be the deciding factor on whether or not to provide ongoing services. Services to care and provide for those that return from war injured is a cost of war and should be our highest priority.

In our reality, however, services that provide long-term care are often handled by non-profits – they understand that the need has not vanished just because the war has slowed to a crawl. Even if we pulled all boots on the ground and declared an absolute end to the war – the needs will continue. We are looking at decades upon decades of the need for services ahead.

Another reason donation dollars fall shy of covering the current demand is that people are unsure where to donate – fearing that their donation dollars are not spent on our veterans. I am frequently asked what organizations are the best. My answer: any organization that has an overhead including administrative expenses and salaries under 15% is an organization that is using the majority of funds raised for the veterans it claims to support. I would be wary of donating to an organization that has an overhead of more than 15%, and there are numerous organizations out there that are well under 15%.

The bottom line is that our veterans, specifically those returning from war injured, will require support above and beyond the VA for a long time and I am grateful there are so many non-profits that have stepped up to fill the gap and will continue to do so long after the war is 'over'.

CHAPTER 6

WARRIOR FOUNDATION
FREEDOM STATION

———⟫•⟪———

A train station is where people go to begin a journey or change course toward a new destination. That was the idea behind Freedom Station USA, a years-long labor of love by Navy wife Sandy Lehmkuhler. While volunteering at Naval Medical Center San Diego in 2004, Mrs. Lehmkuhler was distraught to find that the hospital's injured were in need of some basic quality-of-life items. Spurred by a conversation with two amputees who required special electric razors for shaving, she went on the radio to make a plea for donations and the Warrior Foundation was born. In partnership with the San Diego Council of the U.S. Navy League and under the guidance of its president at the time, retired Navy Commander Jim Bedinger, the Warrior Foundation gained its status as a 501(c)3 nonprofit and has since been dedicated to assisting military men and women who have served our country in the War Against Terrorism. The foundation provides every kind of support imaginable from airfare and hotel rooms for parents coming to their injured children's bedsides, special sunglasses for those whose retinas detached after

21

IED blasts, modified combat boots for prosthetic limbs, and hundreds of plane tickets to send warriors home every year for Christmas.

The day you find out you can no longer be in the military is a hard day.

In her work with the Warrior Foundation, Mrs. Lehmkuhler realized there was a specific group of warriors who needed assistance in one crucial area – the transition from military to civilian life. The day that a Marine, soldier or sailor is told he can no longer be in the military as a result of his or her injuries is a very hard day. This particular group of warriors often enters a period fraught with fear, uncertainty and self-doubt as they await their medical retirement. They told Mrs. Lehmkuhler what they needed was a supportive environment to assist with the transition to civilian life. It is during this critical transition that veterans may fall through the cracks and are at risk of homelessness or joblessness, as evidenced by Vietnam-era veterans who still constitute one of America's largest homeless populations.

The veteran situation is unique in San Diego, one of the largest military industrial complexes in the world. According to a report by the National University System Institute for Policy Research, on any given night, between 1,700 to 2,000 veterans in San Diego sleep in temporary shelters or unsheltered conditions. According to the same report, over any 12-month period, approximately 3,700 veterans in San Diego experience at least one night of homelessness. The economic conditions facing younger veterans are especially difficult, increasing the risk that some will experience prolonged periods of homelessness.

While they may not be in a war zone anymore, injured servicemen and women face new challenges when they return home – the often untold story of coping with injuries, rehabilitation and a transition to civilian life. Mrs. Lehmkuhler was determined to ensure that the men and women who risked their lives for our country would not fall on hard times once they could no longer serve on active duty. She and a group of highly dedicated volunteers made it their passion to deliver what our military members were asking for – a recovery transition center called Freedom Station. This home for heroes would serve as the "missing link" and proactively combat veteran homelessness and joblessness instead of react to it once it was too late. With this vision in mind, Freedom Station celebrated its grand opening in May 2011.

Freedom Station fills the void in San Diego for a transitional environment that servicemen and women often lack as they return to life outside of the military. Troops who have been injured in combat can return home with post-traumatic stress disorder, spinal cord injuries, amputations, traumatic brain injuries, burns and blindness. They find themselves not only coping with injuries but also facing medical retirement and an uncertain new life outside of the Armed Forces. Freedom Station creates a transitional period for acclimating to civilian life and also serves as a "training ground" for challenges ranging from new careers and college entry to monthly budgeting and home buying.

The capital was raised to lease and open the Freedom Station 12-unit housing complex over the course of several years. The property was selected partly for its location just minutes away from Naval Medical Center San Diego which would make it easier for warriors to receive the medical treatment that is so important to their physical and emotional recovery.

The housing complex's design was an equally significant factor. With four apartments and eight cottages all surrounding a central courtyard, Freedom Station was ideally set up to offer the camaraderie that is so crucial to veterans during the transition period. They are able to feel a true sense of community as they recover among their peers, share war stories and know they are supported by others who understand firsthand the harsh realities of war. They are also able to have privacy within their individual living quarters to process and deal with the many changes they are experiencing. Prior to opening the facility, Freedom Station invested a significant amount of capital into making necessary modifications, such as installing wheelchair-accessible ramps and converting several of the apartments to be ADA-compliant. Additionally, each unit was fully furnished and move-in ready, stocked with everything from cleaning supplies to place settings on each dining table. The idea was to shift the warriors from a "barracks mentality" to independent living by including the kinds of household items they would require in daily life.

In addition to providing a home, Freedom Station realized that during this critical time, warriors would also face many decisions that would affect the rest of their lives. They needed help pursuing a career, choosing and enrolling in a college or vocational school, learning how to manage their finances, and locating or purchasing independent housing. Freedom Station provides assistance with and access to professionals and qualified volunteers who assist with educational and career guidance, and other issues relevant to transitioning to civilian life. These services are provided to residents because a helping hand at this point – between the military and the seemingly awesome task of returning to civilian life – is the best way to help solve some of the issues cause by wartime.

While other military housing and transitional facilities exist in the country, there are two key ways in which Freedom Station differs which have ultimately led to its success. As such, the organization hopes to serve as a national model for similar developments. The first differentiator is that most military housing facilities are designed to work with service members after they have already been retired or discharged from the military. In many cases, these veterans may already be having trouble and experiencing "fish out of water" syndrome. Freedom Station understands that the transition needs to take place *before* a military member leaves the service, giving them the necessary time to acclimate. When a warrior finds out he's no longer going to be able to be in the military, for the most part, it takes about a year to be discharged. Instead of allowing them to continue living in the barracks as if active-duty military, Freedom Station saw the value in providing a comforting and supportive environment that would prepare warriors for life outside the military. To not do so in the manner that Freedom Station has constructed would be very hard and stressful on service members; therefore, an average 11-month timeframe for residency is provided. The organization is also unique in that it works directly with Naval Medical Center San Diego, and other local military medical facilities, whose staff and medical personnel are uniquely qualified to identify those most in need of a transitional home.

Secondly, Freedom Station is a hand up, not a hand out. The environment prepares residents for real-world civilian challenges. One of the most vital is having monthly expenses and taking care of those responsibilities. In addition to paying rent, they have utilities to manage, groceries and more. Many military transitional housing facilities are free and do not charge their residents any rent – an unrealistic preparation for real-world living. Although Freedom Station pays the lease on the property every month, residents pay a small amount of rent and are taught how to save and begin to move on.

As evidenced by Freedom Station "graduates" and success stories, the existence of a supportive transitional environment for our military men and women can make all the difference as they begin a new journey outside the service. It is Freedom Station's hope to open additional facilities in the San Diego area thereby expanding to meet the needs of more of our military heroes and ensuring their successful transition to self-sufficient, productive and contributing members of society.

~Sandy Moul

CHAPTER 7

THE STORIES

————— ◦((◦))◦ —————

L ast year when I began interviewing combat injured men for this book, I had no idea what a drastic turn my life would take. I would have never imagined what I would learn from the research conducted for this project nor how that knowledge would alter my opinions on politics and of war.

This project has been at the forefront of my thoughts and life for a solid year. I have carried the recounted versions of eight men's deepest scars in my heart and have walked away from my computer more times than I can count. The responsibility of telling these stories in a way that honors the men who were open enough to share their stories with me is one of the heaviest weights I have ever carried.

CHAPTER 8

FOR THOSE I LOVE

"The last thing I heard was,
'Don't step there,' and then a loud boom."

—————◆—————

"My tattoo, my tattoo," he cried as he lay on the dirt. The corpsman tending to Timothy Read did not tell him that his leg was missing because they thought the tattoo in question was missing as well. Tim's arm was torn to shreds with significant injury to his shoulder, elbow, wrist, and hand. At the time of the injury, there was so much blood covering his arm that the corpsman couldn't see what lay on the one piece of flesh still fully intact. The tattoo read, For Those I Love, I Shall Sacrifice.

Timothy Read joined the Marine Corps on a whim when a recruiter called him to inquire about his post-high school plans. He was seventeen when he enlisted. On his second combat deployment in 2010, he was shot in is his left thigh during a firefight. He refused to go home because he didn't want to leave his brothers behind. Six weeks later, and five months after arriving, Tim stepped on an IED in Marjah, Afghanistan. He lost his left leg above the knee and his right leg was severely damaged. His chest, shoulder, elbow, and wrist were torn to shreds by shrapnel. He also sustained a traumatic brain injury (TBI) and suffers from Post Traumatic Stress Disorder (PTSD).

We were sitting in a San Diego coffee shop for our second interview. About half way through I became painfully aware that the young man had been forever changed by his combat experiences. It wasn't his missing limb or scars that brought that observation so clearly into focus. It was his shaking body, shifty eyes, anxious jumping at every noise and inability to answer a question without taking it somewhere far away from the question I was asking. He was fragile and seemed to have a sense of fearfulness that I have only seen in a few others. His smile appeared forced and his thoughts jumbled.

Tim shared that he had been having a rough time with his transition out of the Marine Corps. His demons had taken over and he had started abusing drugs and alcohol to numb the pain. It's a scenario that is far too common for our troops returning from war. Tim had just returned to Freedom Station after a short stay at a VA facility to detox and stabilize enough emotionally that he no longer posed a threat to himself. He was highly medicated during that interview which accounted for a portion of the change in behavior – but not all of it. It was hard to believe I was sitting across from the same man that I had sat with on a previous occasion – his whole demeanor was different.

Tim's recovery has been long and difficult. Plagued by depression, he turned to drugs and alcohol to ease the physical and emotional pain of his war wounds and demons. The last year has been especially difficult for Tim and his family who often visit to show their support and lift Tim's spirit. Fortunately for Tim, after leaving Balboa Naval Medical Center, he was able to move into a cottage at Freedom Station. Being there has made all the difference in his recovery efforts. Being in a close-knit community of other injured veterans makes it nearly impossible to disguise a setback. Having on-site volunteers who monitor the resident veterans and keep an eye out for trouble also increases the likelihood of early intervention.

During the time spent conducting interviews for this book, I met with Tim on several occasions. His story is important because without the care, assistance and intervention he received as well as the many people who walked through his dark times with him – Tim might be a statistic today. I know people who lost a lot of sleep worrying about and praying for this young man. I watched Tim grow and move forward beautifully over the past year. His one-eighty transformation was made possible, in part, by Freedom Station. Tim married a lovely young lady he met while receiving prosthetic care in Florida. They engaged in a long distance relationship for two years while Tim was in San Diego for rehabilitation and transitioning to civilian life. Tim recently moved to Florida to be with the love of his life; she had a big part in his healing and transformation too.

I chose not to include Tim's full story; he isn't ready to tell it, and I respect that. Tim touched my heart deeply with his goofy expressions and caring personality; both are priceless treasures that I will carry with me for the rest of my days.

CHAPTER 9

THE SCIENTIST

———— ※《◊》※ ————

A t first glance, the average person wouldn't know David Smith is a combat injured Marine Corps veteran. His wounds aren't obvious. David is extremely articulate with an outgoing personality and 'the boy-next-door' good looks. One of the reasons his story is important to share is because he is just that – the boy-next-door. He could be your neighbor.

Raised in Colorado and Texas, he claims Colorado as his home because it's the place he enjoyed the most growing up and he doesn't want to be labeled a Texan. David considers his childhood that of a typical upper-middle class household. Despite his parents' divorce when he was young, he maintained a close loving relationship with both his mom and dad, and spent a great deal of time with both of them.

He grew up playing toy soldiers like many children but joining the military wasn't part of his plan. After high school, David attended New Mexico State University and served as a firefighter on campus. Working side by side with many former Marines that had been to Iraq and Afghanistan in the early years of the war gave him some insight into the realities of being over there. But it wasn't until video of the Nicholas Berg beheading was released that he felt called to join. He couldn't believe that could happen and he wanted to be a part of the organization that put an end to that type of terror.

After three semesters in college, David failed out. His heart wasn't in it – he wanted to be in Iraq. At the age of twenty-one, he joined the United States Marine Corps. Fourteen months after he signed, he was deployed. It would be his first and only deployment.

In David's Words

"One morning I found myself in a recruiter's office. I told him I wanted to join the Marine Corps; I wanted infantry, and I wanted to go to Iraq. I got infantry and was with the 3rd Battalion, 7th Marines.

My dad was all for me joining, but my mom was completely, one hundred and fifty percent against it – so I had that to deal with. My grandfather didn't want me to go to Afghanistan; he knew a lot of guys who had died in Korea and Vietnam. But everyone was supportive right before I deployed.

Boot camp was fun, and school of infantry (SOI) was okay. The fleet sucked. For the first six months I was a new 'boot' Marine, so I got picked on a lot. We had a Sergeant come in who had quite a bit of experience – everyone was a junior Marine compared to him, so nobody overstepped boundaries after he came. Him being there squashed the nonsense.

I didn't get to go to Iraq. I got sent to Afghanistan, which was initially disappointing because I thought it would be boring. I did not hear much about Afghanistan on the news so I assumed not much combat was happening. As we got closer to deploying I learned that there would likely be plenty of excitement. I figured I was prepared for the rigors of combat. The thought never crossed my mind that people I knew were going to die. I thought we were going to go over there, kill some bad guys, and we were all going to come home together. I had a good mindset going in; I knew what I had signed up for. I didn't know what it was going to be like until we got over there – I don't think any of us knew. But I was mentally prepared and physically very prepared. We had a great commanding officer and incredible small unit leaders – they trained us well. We were ready to go.

We flew to Camp Leatherneck and from there went to Delaram to take over for the 3rd Battalion 4th Marines. Nothing happened for a solid three or four weeks – absolutely nothing. For me, that was devastating because I wanted something to happen, y'know? We sat around on base and did patrol missions. We would go out, and the only thing that would happen is we would run over or hit IED's. We knew we were being watched all the time – you just knew – there was this overwhelming sense of being watched. We knew the Taliban drove white vans and motorcycles, so everywhere we went we would see white vans and motorcycles going around our convoys – around us. That was kind of weird. We did over-watch positions in a place that was supposed to be really bad, Buji Bhast Pass, and nothing happened there either.

At the beginning of April, we got to a place called Washir in Northwest Helmand Province. That's when things got a little bit hairy. We set up an observation post in Washir – a village area where a lot of opium is grown. Once there, we started hitting IED's regularly. The outpost the company set up was attacked with small arms fire (SAF), a couple recoilless rifles and we were mortared. I thought this was incredibly fun. This was until Bravo one hit an IED and one of my best friends had the gun turret smash into his face. I began to realize that IED's were a real threat, and we were not invincible. After he was medevaced, we found seven IED's in the 100-meter radius surrounding us. Over the next few days, we began hitting IED's every day or two and started to get tired and a bit concerned. The battalion wanted to know why we were hitting so many IED's. It turns out that this place was a minefield to stop us before we reached the Musa Qala River Valley adjacent to the Sangin district.

There is a Musa Qala City and a Musa Qala River Valley. We were south of the city in the Musa Qala River Valley, technically part of Sangin, that's where we first met up with guys that wanted to fight us. We had already been shot at in Washir, but nobody stuck around. It was like they were just testing our tactics.

When we went into Musa Qala the first time, we kind of got it handed to us. We only had half a company of guys, and there were an estimated 200-300 hardened Taliban fighters in the area. We were going through this little valley, and every time we moved we would get shot at. We started to find tactical things that we didn't expect; sand models of the area, medical stations, and an elaborate tunnel system. For the first time – for me – we were getting some. It wasn't like little pop-shots here and there; we were actually taking some fire. It was kind of weird for me. That all happened in Musa Qala one.

We all came back and re-grouped. We knew where the enemy was now, and we knew they were in the town of Regay in the valley. So we went in as a full company and in the first thirty minutes of being there one of the combat replacements in CAAT white was killed. When that happened – it was completely surreal. I was watching them through the tow missile system and then all of the sudden this guy; he fell. A few minutes later when they came back the corpsman got out of the truck, silent, covered in blood.

I never processed that until after I got home. I just sat there, and I knew that it had happened but at the time it just didn't feel real. That night was a solemn night. No one talked to each other. It woke us all up. Before that we had just been screwing up the Taliban. But now, it was like, oh – we died here – like you can die here. That first time in Musa Qala we killed like sixty of them. We were really getting some, and now it was their turn. This guy, our guy, had just died. The next morning our company call sign was changed to vengeance, and we were all told that we were to kill as many of these guys as we could.

The next morning I had my little claim to fame. I was a Tow Gunner by trade, and so I was watching the hill where the platoon had taken fire from when the guy had gotten killed the day before. There was a group of men up there. I started watching them at six in the morning. I could not engage them until they had weapons. Another one of our platoons and some scout snipers pushed out towards that area around seven and started getting close to the hill around eight. The groups of men were being directed around the area by a guy in a white man dress. I could see they were wearing some type of vests but could not see any weapons. When our guys started getting close these guys split into two big groups and started running toward a van, pulling weapons out and setting a mortar up. When that happened, I asked for clearance and the captain told me to smoke them. I took the shot and killed at least eight of them although I only ended up finding four torsos. The hit was at 3967 meters; I engaged them right at the range limit of where it's even possible to shoot. I had a direct hit. It was the best feeling I had ever had to this point in my life. I know at least a couple of them had been involved in killing the guy the day before, so I felt all right. We started taking machine gun fire immediately after from an adjacent tree line and a couple minutes later so my excitement didn't go away.

The next couple of days the sound of combat was constant, we were really giving it to them, very high kill counts. We all did our jobs and made our commanders proud. About a week later we came back from a hellacious patrol where we were harassed constantly. On the way back to the makeshift outpost though I don't think we even got shot at – we were exhausted. They were bringing a cold water truck in with an ammo resupply. The first thing I remember, coming back to the command post, is there were four or five trucks that had hit IED's. We found out that the area we had set up on was covered in IED's. I remember getting back up there, and that was real weird – there were blown up pieces of trucks everywhere. Injured guys sitting in the blown up trucks and the radio was constantly chattering. Troops in contact everywhere.

The supply guys started coming in, and it didn't really click in my mind that I shouldn't be walking next to this truck. But I ran over there. I was all excited because there was cold water in this truck, and we hadn't had any cold water for a couple of days. The truck hit an IED. The driver lost his legs and one guy is still in the hospital; he's been there four years. After the IED had gone off, I was looking around dazed. I saw a body just slam on the ground. He was still alive, – he probably weighed 110 lbs – that IED just picked his body up and threw him high and far to where I had slammed down. I looked around and saw this body just slam down on the ground next to me. I tried to help out as best I could then lost consciousness. I woke up later – I don't really remember the next two or three weeks. I was in a hospital in Afghanistan for a week or two then I was in Germany for two and a half weeks. I don't remember that time – it's like lost time. After that, I went to Walter Reed for a little bit and then to Balboa. I didn't lose limbs; Balboa has a focus on amputees. I had a serious head injury – I got that taken care of. Life sucked pretty bad right after I came back because I didn't want to be home.

My guys were all in combat. I guess I was lucky though – after I had got hurt, one of the guys from the company stepped on an IED and got torn up pretty badly, and then our radio operator got torn up, our staff sergeant got shot – all these guys from the platoon got hurt and didn't see much more combat after that. In Sangin, they got it pretty good a couple of times but nothing like Musa Qala. The worst part about the whole thing – the day after I left a couple of guys got killed but nobody that I was close to got killed until after I came home. The night of the memorial we had for the guys who died – my squad leader got killed by four drunk Marines outside the gate of Twenty-nine Palms right after our memorial for the guys who got killed in Afghanistan. A week before that a guy I went to boot camp with got killed in a car accident. My best friend rolled his truck and died. That was the last straw. I didn't want to be around anymore after that.

I was taking a bunch of medications that the doctors had given me and was addicted to painkillers – I didn't need them at the amount I was taking. I was a mess. I think that's a real problem in the hospitals. I don't think the doctors know how to monitor or measure the level of pain we go through or the way to best treat it. The amount of medications I was taking was insane. I woke up taking pain meds and ended my day taking them. I was messed up for awhile – addicted to pain meds. Then I woke up one day and just quit. But I had wasted an entire year of my life; a whole year living in the barracks in San Diego doing nothing. Not doing what I should have been doing. Not hanging out with the guys that I should have been hanging out with.

Then I met Sandy about a year after I got to San Diego. I met her right when I got told that I was being retired from the Marine Corps. That wasn't something that I wanted to happen. I kind of had a plan of going on – in the Marine Corps. I got told I was going to be retired and shortly after that my friend, Povas, told me about Sandy. He was the only friend I had at the time that wasn't a complete nightmare of a mess. He had been injured about a year before I had, and so he had already gone through the shitty parts of coming home after you're hurt. We became really good friends. He moved into Freedom Station and right after that I decided that's where I needed to go.

Living in the barracks just wasn't conducive to realizing that life goes on after that. I mean you got to think about it – coming from combat where you saw guys get torn up, saw people get killed, and you killed people then you are living around a bunch of guys who are just ripped to shreds. I don't like how the Marine Corps does that. They should not put everyone in the barracks – a cramped barracks – and especially because its run by the Navy – the Navy guys who – they have no idea what it's like. The Wounded Warrior Battalion, at that time, was run by a bunch of reservists and those guys have no idea. The way the Marine Corps was handling that – it was a mess. But we muddled through, got a lot of Page Eleven's – got in trouble often – but it was cool.

I remember one morning formation after my injury; this Sergeant – the worst Sgt. I have ever seen in the Marine Corps – was yelling at one guy. He had lost a leg and wasn't able to run yet. The Sgt. yelled at him and let him know he should be running to the formation. Everyone was quiet – nobody said anything. I went off on the Sgt. He kept telling me I was over-stepping my bounds, I was a Corporal at the time. This Sgt. hadn't done anything in his Marine Corps career close to what this guy had done. I told him that in front of the junior Marines, and he said I needed to calm down. I got in his face, grabbed him by the cammies and pulled him close to my face and said, "Don't fuck with me." Then I let the Sgt. go. He emailed my unit, which was still deployed in Afghanistan, and told them what a shit-bag Marine I was. My command responded letting the Sgt. know that they had just given me a meritorious promotion. I ended up not getting that promotion for a few months because the Sgt. held it up until my command returned home and got the full story. It's that kind of stuff at the Wounded Warrior Battalion that didn't make any sense to me. It doesn't make sense to mess with a bunch of injured guys.

I got approved to move to Freedom Station – I don't think the command wanted to approve me – at the time I was a nightmare. I wouldn't listen to anybody; I was punching people and didn't care about anything. I'm sure they thought I was out of my mind. I guess I was. I was drunk almost one hundred percent of the time; in the middle of the day and the morning, I was either drunk or on pills. Then I moved out and as soon as I moved it was like this veil was lifted off of me and I could see that life was going to be normal again. When I moved, I started going to school and living life. Even after I moved though, I still didn't respect authority. I was told to dress in cammies for formations and would conveniently forget. Once I knew I was getting out of the Marine Corps – I didn't trust them anymore, these weren't the guys I was in combat with – I just couldn't care less about some guy telling me to shave my face. I just didn't respect these guys – with the exception of Lt Col Bleidistel; he was the only person in that whole detachment that believed in me besides Mr. Cheney and Jack Lyon. If it weren't for Lt Col Bleidistel I wouldn't have been able to go to school. He believed in me and he made it happen."

David left San Diego after residing at Freedom Station for nine months. He moved to Texas to attend the University of North Texas. He began as an economics major, but his path would eventually take him in a different direction.

"I wanted to go into the stock market. I was at the University sitting there with a bunch of frat boys and sorority girls, and I hated every second of it. It wasn't challenging. I was sitting in classrooms and regurgitating information that anybody can find on the internet. After the first semester I switched to biology which was my interest the first time I went to college. I started taking biology and chemistry classes. About six months after I started at Texas I met my mentor, Dr. Guenter Gross, a world-renowned neuroscientist. I started doing research with him and toxicology studies. I was most interested though in traumatic brain injury. We came up with a model to mimic a TBI. It's ground breaking research. I attended Scholar's Day at my university, and I submitted a poster with my research on it. I didn't realize how big this was until that day. I kept hearing Dr. Gross say that this was the frontier, the future in research, but I figured he had to tell me that. On Scholar's Day there were many great posters, but I ended up winning. I won a fifteen hundred dollar travel grant. I didn't end up getting the grant due to a technicality – I wasn't in the Honors College.

Winning that competition gave me confidence in what we were doing, so I submitted my research to a neuroscience conference in Germany and was selected to present it at that conference. I couldn't afford to travel to Germany but knew how important it was to get this research out there. I made a call to Freedom Station and they handled the travel expenses for me – they know how important this research is too – especially for our combat-injured guys. During the time in between those two events, I had been published twice for research on TBI and an anti-malarial drug. The research started to get attention and I was asked to present it again in Washington D.C. Learning more about TBI is important, we don't know enough. Essentially what I do is quantify the effects of TBI and how long it takes for cells to recover from TBI. I am thinking of transferring to the University of Texas, Dallas to do my Ph.D. They have a center for brain health there. I would like to make devices to put into the brain that can more accurately detect what's going on in there. That's my goal – we will see what happens.

I would like to see a University pick up my research model and use it to look at pharmacological intervention. After you suffer a traumatic brain injury, you have to take all these medications: sleep medications, pain medications, SSRI's. You end up on so many medications. I want to look at how their interactions with each other and

the brain affect the recovery of nerve cell networks. If you are imped-
ing some repair mechanism that the brain is trying to do – you are
delaying recovery from a brain injury, and you might even be doing
permanent damage. From what I've seen in my studies if you get even
a small brain injury, the effects of that are not going to go away. You
might recover gradually over time, but you will never recover completely. With my brain injury – I don't know what happened to me. I
was just filing out an application last night and looking over my previous college grades. I had a 1.75 GPA before starting college again,
and now I have a 3.5 GPA even with five F's on my transcript. I don't
know what happened to me – I think my brain injury – Afghanistan
as a whole – woke me up to living. I wasn't living before. I'd like to
see my research translate into clinical research. Someone needs to
work on this for five to ten years and then that might happen. If nobody does, that's fine too. As soon as I have my Ph.D., I will start it
right back up again. It's a great method. We will see what happens.

I want people to know about the horror of war. I find myself
caught up in reading comments to posts or articles online – I don't
know why I do, but I do. And, I get angry when I read ones that say,
"They signed up for it – how come they didn't know?"

I want to grab those people and tell them that you can't possibly
know what's going to happen – you can sign up for it all you want.
Everybody is a little bit different, and people that sign up for war
have a warrior in them – there's something in them that just drags
them over there. So when people say "they signed up for it," I understand I signed up for it, but they don't understand the honor or the
altruism associated with doing it. The ultimate form of altruism is to
sacrifice your life. It's against every evolutionary principle in biology.
That a Marine will jump on a grenade to save another Marine –
without even thinking about it – just does it. I've seen stuff like that
happen. People don't understand what that's like. You can never understand unless you go there. The only way to get close is to hear
stories first hand from us. I read a book recently about the Spartans.
When the Spartans came back to Sparta or Greece as a whole, the
townspeople would bring them in and they would all sit down, and

the Warriors would talk about all of their experiences. Everyone would be completely open with it. No one was saying, "I'm sorry," there was no hero worship, nobody was crying about it; the people would just listen. They listened. They learned from the experiences, and it helped everyone to understand each other after a battle. It was an open discussion – the ugly included.

I don't talk about my experiences with these college kids because the second I do I get, "Oh, I'm so sorry." I don't want you to be sorry for me. I don't want anybody to be sorry for me at all. It doesn't help anything. I also don't want you to say, "You're a hero," because I'm not. I'm just a regular guy. The term hero has been so overused that it has no meaning anymore. Everyone is a hero now. If you do any- thing – you're a hero. It's just not true. My definition of a hero is much different. For instance – a basketball star gets labeled a hero but leaves a game because he has cramps or bangs a knee too hard. How is he a hero? We have all of these parades and ceremonies on Veteran's Day, and you have people bowing down worshipping veter- ans. The guys that are the real deal, they don't want that. It's the guys that have never seen combat that want that stuff.

It's the same with the VA. I had this conversation with a con- gressman and a VA director, and they asked me what I thought the biggest problem was with the VA. My answer to that is easy; it's the veterans themselves. That's the biggest problem with the VA. Every time I go down there I sit next to some guy who is trying to tell me the best or easiest way to get more money. It should not be that way. I sat down next to a guy one day and I was wearing a brace; he im- mediately asked me if I was getting paid for the brace. No, I'm not getting paid for the brace. I already have a disability rating that's more than fair. The guy proceeds to tell me how much I can get for wearing the brace, what paperwork to fill out and who to talk to. Then he gets up and walks away. Every single time I go to the VA it's the same – someone telling me how to get more money. It infuriates me because I have to use the VA. I go down there and can't make an appointment because there's fifty people in front of me who don't have a single injury from combat or even from the military – they just twisted their knee at some point in life, and they blame it on the military. It's being used as welfare, and it shouldn't be that way. I feel that this hero-worshipping culture just plays into that. It allows these guys to clog the channels with unnecessary claims. I don't agree with it. It's a strange thing for me to say, but there are a lot fewer heroes than people think.

A lot has changed since my injuries, my time in the military. Although I still have a close relationship with my family, and my mom would say she knows everything about me; I hide the bad and tell her what I think she wants to hear. It's easier that way. I didn't realize that our relationship had changed until a few years after my injury. I didn't realize that I had changed. During the year I went through abusing pain meds I was a lunatic. Once I cleaned up, I started noticing things that were different. My wife said I was different, my mom would probably say the same. I think I hold stuff in to protect myself – not others. I don't care if people know what I did; if someone has an altered opinion of me based on something I had to do in an austere environment – I really don't care. I'm not going to change that opinion. But if I can avoid having someone say "I'm sorry," then I will avoid that at all costs. I will give you a great example. I had a class with this kid, a civilian kid, and I started going to the gym with him and hanging out with him. I never told him anything, never said anything about the military or my injury. When he asked what I did before I just told him I dropped out of college and kept quiet about the rest. One day I asked him if he wanted to get a beer. We went out to my car, and he saw my Purple Heart license plates. He asked if it was my dad's car and I told him it was mine. Then he asked, and I had to tell him. Whenever I have to tell someone what happened, I always preface it with the strong desire to not have sympathy from them. I don't want to deal with emotion – I don't like seeing people sad – most of the time it's hard to see people sad about trivial things. I've seen things to be sad about.

The biggest things that have changed about me – that's a hard question to answer. That makes me have to think about myself. I'm trying to get rid of what people have told me. I definitely have a temper that's difficult to control sometimes which is kind of crazy because I go from zero to a hundred. I'm a pretty relaxed person and I'm usually calm. But if something irks me a certain way; instead of recognizing it and calming myself down – its just bam – I'm mad. This is an issue for me, so now I stay away from things that cause my anger.

The other thing that changed for me is my outlook on life. Before I joined the Marine Corps I was partying all the time. I was in a fraternity my first time in college and that's probably why I failed out. I was really into myself, I guess. But after I was in Afghanistan, that changed. I was talking to a buddy of mine about this recently. In the Marine Corps you can be suffering on a hike or suffering because someone just died or lost a leg, or suffering because you just killed someone and that was the first person you ever killed, you are suffering in your head. Then you realize that you are suffering, but everyone around you feels the same way and if everyone else feels the same way there's no reason for me to lag behind. I had to perform in front of these guys, and we all have to keep our spirits up – keep our positivity and get through it together. I never had anything like that before. I didn't ever have anything like that, never played sports in high school where you had to care about others and put other people before yourself. On a deeper level – for myself – I didn't turn to religion, but I did start to see a bigger picture. Everything in life seems to work out the way it's supposed to. As long as you're a pretty good person and try to do as many good things as possible, good things will happen eventually. We just had another guy from 3/7 kill himself. We all come together. I tell my friends if they call me and they are having a rough time, today is rough but tomorrow it could be completely different. Life can be gone so fast it's incredible. This can all be gone so fast; every day has to be treated like a good day. We just have to live like that – all of us. I think if we did there would be less dickheads in the world. I don't know what the answer to the suicide epidemic is – I wish I knew. I just don't understand it. I've lost so many people that I have become emotionless to death. I guess that's part of the deal for a lot of us."

David was my first interview and it was eye opening. The fact that he has gone through the horrors of war, fallen down and gotten back up stronger than before is not only a testament to his mental strength but also to the organization that helped him overcome the darkest days following his return home. Although he maintained a tough exterior while sharing his story with me, I could feel the pain behind much of what he recounted. I believe David will continue to do well and will most likely go on to accomplish his dream of helping to further our understanding of the impact of Traumatic Brian Injuries and how to properly treat them.

CHAPTER 10

THE MECHANIC

———⟫•«⟪———

Wrenching on cars, surfing and golfing all with one arm; Michael "Mike" Spivey will not only tell you it's possible, but he will also show you it's possible to excel in all of those areas – with one arm. With his kind eyes and engaging personality, my interview with Mike felt more like catching up with an old friend and for hours I got lost in his story. After the first few minutes together, it was apparent to me that his attitude towards life and living plays a major role in his ability to move forward, despite his injuries.

Mike was born at Camp Lejeune and grew up in Texas. Joining the Marine Corps wasn't part of his initial plan. He moved out of his parents' house when he was seventeen. He worked in various industries and settled in at a retail establishment where he remained for three years. He started college and picked up another job to help pay for tuition. Money got tight, and there were rumors of his company closing, so he took a semester off. His journey to the Marine Corps started at that point.

In Mike's Words

"I started talking to family members about joining the military. Most of my family had served at least four years in the service. The added benefit of having college paid for if I served for four years was tempting, but it took me about six months and many recruiter office drive-bys before I made a final decision. I had done a lot of research and I knew what I wanted to do. I wanted to be a combat engineer because 1- you get to play with explosives and 2- if you aren't playing with explosives, you're building stuff. Because I had a GED and only a little bit of college, the recruiter said I would have to pass the ASVAB before I could request that job. I think he was skeptical of my abilities. I went down and took the test and got one of the highest scores, so the recruiter said I could be whatever I wanted to be. I wanted to be a combat engineer. The recruiter tried to sway me in different directions but they all sounded like office jobs, and I don't like paper. I like to be outside; I like manual labor.

I went in as a combat engineer. The first two years I was on an MEU (Marine Expeditionary Unit) going a couple of places helping to build schools, bridges and clinics in Southeast Asia. I deployed to Iraq in 2007; it wasn't that bad. We took a couple of pop shots here and there. My truck hit an IED, but by that time we had up-armored vehicles. It didn't do much damage, so we just kept pushing. I came back from Iraq and transferred to Camp Pendleton and stayed around there for about nine months then I deployed to Afghanistan with the 3/5. I made it about three months. Like I said – I got to play with explosives; the bad side to that coin is that I walked around with a metal detector searching for them.

At first we were shadowing the guys from the previous unit that we were replacing, trying to learn from them. Originally the unit I was with wanted to run patrols like they had in Iraq, but it didn't take them long to realize that wasn't going to work. We took contact the first day out. After the first week, I made the comment that I just wanted to make it out of there alive and with these guys I probably wouldn't make it to my thirtieth birthday. Eventually, we started figuring things out. Things were going well, and my NAVman and I were able to pick out the IEDs and ambushes before they could get us.

On December 10, three days before my birthday and after about three months – I missed one. It hit my NAV man too; he was directly on top of it. He lost both knees and his elbow. He was always right over my shoulder; we were right next to each other. We joked if one of us got hit the other would too because we were right on top of each other. And that's how it happened.

I didn't lose my hand at first; the blast had just severed the radial nerve from the elbow to the wrist and about six inches of the medial nerve. The blast broke the radial bone in multiple places and blew off a finger and several knuckles and I had burns on what was left. I also took a bunch of shrapnel to my lower back and both legs. It took two baseball-sized chunks out of my back on either side of my spine, and they had to fuse a couple vertebrae together. My legs were peppered with shrapnel – some so deep they resembled holes in a bowling ball almost costing me my left leg. My ears were shot; my hearing was completely gone in one and about forty percent gone in the other. I ended up in Germany for my birthday. It was a hard time. They picked us up in a chopper and took us to a base in Afghanistan. While I was on the bird, they gave me pain meds and I was kind of in and out. I'd wake up and then they would knock me out again to wash out my wounds. When I arrived in Germany, I was totally disoriented. My memories were of limping to the bird, to going into an operating room in Afghanistan and then waking up in Germany. I was freaking out because they wouldn't tell me anything about McCloud, my NAV man. When I got hit, they kept him behind me. They wouldn't even let me turn around to see how he was. They said he was talking and said something to me but with my hearing being gone I guess I didn't hear him. They wouldn't tell me if he was okay or alive. Then right before midnight on my birthday, McCloud came out of the OR and the nurses took me around the corner to another wing to see him.

It all happened fast. The next morning they moved me from Germany to Bethesda and then here to San Diego on the fifteenth.

So I was hit on the tenth and was in San Diego by the fifteenth. Mainly because they were trying to save my arm, and all the hand specialists are here. McCloud stayed in Bethesda for a few months before he made it over here, because he had leg trauma doctors there. When I got here the doctors were already on Christmas leave, so for the first two weeks I had wash-outs every day in the OR to prevent infection. Soon they stopped taking me to the OR and started doing the wash-outs in my room which allowed me to actually eat. I had lost so much weight from being over there and being prepped to go to the OR. When they weighed me on the sixteenth I was about one hundred and ten pounds.

The doctors returned from Christmas holiday, and I could tell by the look on my doctor's face that it wasn't going to be good news. He started talking in doctor jargon, and I interrupted him and asked if I would ever be able to make a fist and he said probably not. I immediately told him to cut it off, give me a prosthetic, something I can work with. I've known people with amputations and even have a family member that had lost an arm, so I knew it was possible to go on and have a productive life even without a hand. After saying that I had to see shrinks and talk to other guys that had lost limbs, they made me watch some video. Instead I watched 127 Hours. The guy in it was still rock-climbing even with a prosthetic.

I did talk to guys in my situation; one guy had a limb salvage and the other was an amputee. The limb salvage guy was still dealing with surgeries and stuff four years and fifty surgeries later and could transfer a pen from one hand to another – not much more. I didn't want to go through that many surgeries. The day after talking to the shrink and the amputee, who had lost an arm and a leg, I told the doctor to cut it off. My mom didn't want me to cut it off, but what's the point of saving it if it doesn't do anything. I wanted to get back to living life. So the first of the year came, and we did it.

I was living in the barracks at the time learning how to use my prosthetic, but the barracks isn't like real life. I had a small room that was mine but still ate at the chow hall and someone would come clean for me – I realized that I wasn't going to learn how to be independent that way. I was able to move into Freedom Station and that made a big difference in my recovery. Living at Freedom Station I had my own place with a kitchen. I had to learn how to clean house and make food with my prosthetic. Within three weeks of having my prosthetic and living at Freedom Station, I was showing my therapist how to do things instead of being taught. I also picked up some tricks from other amputees during outings that we attended together. Having the outside experience of learning how to use your prosthetic is invaluable.

I don't use my prosthetic for a lot of things that I do. I can't surf with it because the strap makes my arm go numb, and I can't lift more than thirty or so pounds with it. The past few years they have started working with a robotic arm, and I think that works better for some things. The technology has improved but it's not quite there yet where one arm can work for everything. It takes a lot of work to learn how to use any of them so that the benefit outweighs the trouble. At the end of the day, using my prosthetic or not using the prosthetic depends on what I am doing. It works well for some things, but for other things it's easier to just not to use it. Trying to hold a piece of metal and using a drill press is a challenge without the prosthetic. Golfing with the prosthetic didn't work out that great so I asked one of the golf academy coaches to teach me how to swing one-handed – I got lucky because one of the coaches ended up in a cast and had had to teach himself how to play one-handed.

My buddy Derek and I would play golf a lot, we would get asked what handicap we were and would immediately answer that we were missing an arm. You could always see the face of whoever asked the question go white at first – it was actually a good icebreaker. We got a lot of great laughs out of it. Being around an amputee makes a lot of people uncomfortable. We have all this political correctness stuff to deal with and people are scared to ask us about it. It wasn't that long ago that your life was just kind of over if you were an amputee, and I don't think society has caught up with the times like the amputee or injured community has.

When the Vietnam guys came back, they started implementing programs so injured guys could still live a full life. It's the Vietnam guys who really began to pave the way for programs to be put in place for injured guys. For our group of veterans the stigmatism of someone with a disability isn't something that nobody wants to talk about – it's not so hush-hush. Now we just try to figure out how to do the same things we used to do – the same things people without missing limbs can do. It's not that we can't do it – it's just that we have to figure out a modified way to do it. Everything we do is just a little bit harder. I have to think about things now before I do them, but I can still do things. If I'm carrying groceries in from my truck, I might have to make two trips instead of getting it all in one trip, but I can still carry my groceries into the house.

Being at Freedom Station has given me a lot of opportunities. I've learned how to network and am able to be around people from many different industries. I have learned how to live independently again while forming friendships with the other guys there. Being there helped me to feel more comfortable around people. By slowly being introduced to golf events and things like that where I was around different people, it helped me find my comfort zone and adapt to being looked at differently out in the real world. It gave me time to figure out what my next step was. While I was there, I started looking for a house to buy. That took a little longer than expected because I wanted a place with some space. Sandy helped me choose a realtor that understood my unique needs, and she made sure I didn't get taken advantage of. I had never bought a house before and there was a lot to learn during the process.

People will ask you basic questions all the time when you're out there. After awhile, you can tell where the conversation's heading and you kind of just roll with it and wait for the person to go through a 'chapter' to get to the question they want to ask you. In a roundabout way, Freedom Station helped me transition to the real word. Talking about my story and some of the guilt I have was really hard for me to do. I could never fully tell the story. But being out around civilians, I have gotten to the point where I can tell it. I can get past it, and I don't know if I could have or would have gone out and done that on my own. In a way, it was like group therapy without really being in a group therapy session.

There are a lot of opportunities through connections at Freedom Station to do internships or go to school. I got in trouble for golfing too much while I was supposed to be recovering and planning for the future. But I've met so many people while golfing and been offered more jobs than I can count. I wasn't sure at that time what I wanted to be when I 'grew up'. I was doing my own thing surfing, golfing and working on cars – that was my rehabilitation. After that, I think they understood that I wasn't ready to commit to something until I knew the direction I wanted to go in. I was a combat engineer, that's what I wanted to do, that's what I knew how to do, but it's kind of hard to do that with one arm."

These days Mike is showing his Roadster at car shows and just picked up a new project. He also spends a great deal of time fixing up his new house. With the help of friends and family, he is completely remodeling it to make it a place where he can do everything without having to take two trips.

He fell in love with snowboarding and is currently training for the Paralympics. Mike still spends time at Freedom Station and with the friends he made while living there. Sandy continues to be somewhat of a surrogate mother, and Mike is still trying to decide what he wants to be when he grows up. I suspect he is living his dream already, and I have little doubt that we will see his name pop up in the world of classic car restoration as well as snowboarding in the very near future.

CHAPTER 11

THE STUDENT

———— ⇒»(())«⇐ ————

Povas Miknaitis has the face of an angel, but you can tell there is a virulent story hiding behind his beautiful smile and charismatic personality. Born and raised in Elmhurst, Illinois, where his parents still live in his childhood home, he is the youngest of five siblings. He admits to getting in trouble often as a child and attributes that to his parents' overly strict house rules. Although his parents were tough on him, he speaks of his mother fondly recalling her cooking every single meal every day of his childhood. Povas learned to cook from his mom, and his knack for fixing things came from his father who was a microchip engineer for Motorola during Povas' youth.

Povas was drawn to serve on multiple levels. With his two older brothers in the Marine Corps, he felt the pull to follow in their footsteps. The events of 9/11 turned that desire into an obligation to serve his country. Coming from a strong Christian background, he also believed it was his duty to join. He believed that if he didn't return that was okay because he knew where he was going if he were to die, and it would therefore allow other young men a chance at life and getting their lives together.

Povas joined the Marine Corps on a reconnaissance contract in

2006. Before going in, he asked his brothers for advice on how to get through the rigors of boot camp. They advised him to lay low and keep himself out of the spotlight. Povas did the opposite. His brothers added to that by sending him letters while in boot camp addressed to 'Sergeant Miknaitis'. With his drill instructor handing out the mail, that didn't go over well; it kept him in the spotlight.

After boot camp and infantry school, Povas' excellence and skills allowed him the opportunity to take the indoc for a spot in a Scout Sniper Platoon. He passed the indoc and immediately began training to be a Scout Sniper in Twenty-nine Palms, California. He made his first deployment to Iraq in 2008 operating within the scout sniper community of 3rd BN 4th Marines Scout Sniper Platoon and, after more training and Scout Sniper School in Hawaii, then deployed to Afghanistan in October 2009.

The violence and trauma of his story are still vivid and painful. Often the reader will notice his story slips from past to present tense at various places as he relives it. I've left these shifts largely unedited allowing the reader to relive it with him.

In Povas' Words

"October 2009 we were replacing a unit that had gotten totally jacked up by the Taliban. They had taken so many casualties that they wouldn't leave friendly lines. You are supposed to take patrols out daily and patrol the surrounding area. They would not leave the area immediately surrounding the FOB, basically just patrolling the wall. They couldn't afford to lose anybody else. My unit was taking over in Nowzad in Helmand Province; it was entirely different than I thought a war zone would be. The U.S. had dropped leaflets on Nowzad that said to get out, and that if anyone was still there when we came in they would be assumed to be with the insurgency. The whole town was left abandoned and the only people that remained were insurgents. They ended up booby-trapping the entire city; they had put IED's everywhere. We knew they had. They put so many IED's that they didn't even remember where they all were; the insurgents were getting blown up by their own IED's almost every day.

They would come in at night and place bombs – IEDs – all around. Our FOB only inhabited a small area of the city of Nowzad.

While we were busy patrolling and looking for IED's, the insurgency – the Taliban – was out placing IED's and setting ambushes. While performing our change over with the former occupying unit; it was crazy because you would be on one side of a street and wouldn't take fire, but the second you crossed to the other side of the road you were going to hit an elaborate ambush. The Taliban were very coordinated with their attacks.

Afghanistan was a different animal; it was Taliban we were fighting. It was obvious they had been doing this for years; that was how they grew up. Kids were trained by their dads; it was passed from generation to generation; it was their culture."

Povas began to shake a bit, and I could see the color drain from his face. I knew this was an area he didn't feel comfortable talking about, and we took a break and moved from the coffee house we had begun our interview in to a quiet, grassy area overlooking the San Diego Marina. After some small talk, Povas said he was ready to continue.

"When we did our official changeover, our team got split up and spread across the AO (Area of Operation) that 3/4 was operating in. 3/4 wasn't just in Nowzad; they were also in Sangin and a few other provinces. I think we had three or four teams, each team consisting of four guys. We were put on the QRF (Quick Reaction Force) basically for the infantrymen of Lima Company. Initially, we weren't officially doing any reconnaissance missions.

Usually, it would start off with an IED while guys were out on patrol. They would hit an IED then all of the sudden a complex ambush of machine gun fire and mortars came from everywhere. So we got guys with a broken truck stuck out there. When that happened we would get called over and got there quick. We would set up and gain back control of the situation, laying down some aggressive fire for the squad that was under ambush. That would happen a few times a week. It was insane getting mortars dropped on you or coming around a corner and just barely missing an RPG. It's close fire that training can only scratch the surface of. It's not normal for humans to run towards danger, but we did regularly, and it's like 'Holy shit, I can die any moment right now.'

Eventually, our command started pushing us out into other parts of the city. We were doing reconnaissance in areas that the U.S. hadn't seen since the beginning of the war because the Taliban were so strong in those areas. The enemy had pushed back every unit that was there before us. The area was surrounded by mountains and when things got too hot in the city the Taliban would retreat to the mountains.

We went out one night to a part of the city that hadn't been explored since the beginning of the war in Afghanistan. We went foot mobile because that's the only way to sneak out there. If we were on a truck, the Taliban would see us coming. We set up in a house for observation. We had an engineer with us which was annoying because we could have swept for mines ourselves; we knew how to do that. That night the engineer said he was glad to be out with us because if anything happened we could put the shit down and he would be safe. That pissed me off. I told him that we could all die at any time and he couldn't let his guard down. Inside I was thinking – shit this guy is too complacent, he thinks he is okay because he is with us.

I was one of the senior members for our Op that night. Our Team Leader realized that we didn't have eyes on the right objective, and he calls it in. We decide to move locations first thing the next morning. We were moving just a couple of houses down and we used an alley to get there. We are walking through the alley and there's a hole into this courtyard. We crawl through it and go to the back door of the house under an awning we're setting up to enter the building. Like a typical American house, there's a patio area with stone pillars holding up a wooden trellis over the little back patio area. Our engineer sweeps the door to make sure it is not booby-trapped (I only see this out of the corner of my eye). The one thing that bothered me during training to sweep for mines was that the engineers training us told us not to turn the sweeper up to its highest sensitivity. They said if it was all the way up it would detect a paper clip and we would spend all day walking around paperclips. I was like, 'Hey, turn it up; I will

walk around paperclips all day. I mean, I will take a twenty-mile de-
tour if it means not getting my legs blown off.'

Our engineer sweeps the door and says it's clear. I'm standing under that trellis in the back patio near the middle pillar looking back
at the courtyard near the hole we came through just keeping security
watch. My buddy, Josh Sweeny, kicks the door in and takes one step
in, and there's an IED in the floor. It goes off, and I'm right there in
the midst of this vast explosion.

The next thing I remember is seeing shit fly everywhere and being on the ground. I regain consciousness and look around, and
people are fucking crying everywhere, it's shitty to hear them tore up.
I get up and realize I can't talk, and I'm wondering why the fuck I
can't talk. I feel my face and there's blood all over. I shove some gauze
in real quick and get over to my buddy, Sweeny, and his legs are fucking gone. A couple of teammates are putting tourniquets on Sweeny
to keep him from bleeding out; they were able to get him stable. I
assist in making sure everything is tight and that he's not bleeding
anywhere else. I finish wrapping up my face as I run over to assist my
injured teammates, not as serious as Sweeny, but they have huge
chunks missing out of their arms and legs. We get to them, apply
pressure dressings and help fix them up then we immediately radio
in. I was the second radio operator but couldn't call anything because
my mouth didn't work. Our primary was radioing in trying to get our
QRF to get us out of there. There is a lot of yelling and chaos – radio
asking if QRF is coming. In the meantime, I'm posting up security
and going from guy to guy making sure to keep them conscious because you have to treat for shock. Even though you've stopped the
bleeding, you have to make sure they want to keep fighting for their
lives. If you let them just sit there with their thoughts, they can die.

Then our engineer disappears; I didn't know where the fuck he
went at the time. One of the guys in our platoon who wasn't hurt was
curled up in a ball crying and shaking; looking around at the devastation was surreal. I found out that our engineer had run out to the
street to wave in our QRF so they knew where we were at – but they
already knew ("he's fucking dumb"), they had our grid coordinates.

You aren't supposed to go out on your own because you can cause another casualty; he wasn't thinking – he was caught up in the moment. So, we're waiting for our QRF and the radio operator said they were right around the corner and all of a sudden we hear an explosion and see body parts; there's a fucking leg in the air. They hit an IED trying to get to us.

Over the top we have Air Force and we are talking to them on the radio trying to get PJ's (para jumpers) to jump in. They are trying to clear it but can't because the area is so hot – it was two hours before QRF got to us. Luckily we kept everyone left in our compound alive. Finally, once the QRF's got to us, I grabbed Sweeny's stretcher. I was carrying him out asking where the other QRF was hit and look around and just see fucking blood and body parts splattered everywhere. We are getting our casualties loaded up in the vehicles and they see I'm fucked-up too. They're like, 'Are you okay? You been treated?' They put me on a stretcher and we got driven to an evacuation point because the helicopters couldn't get to where we were hit at. Our convoy struck more IED's on the way out. From there the Brit's pick us up. In the helicopter, I hear everything. They are working on Sweeny, Gritter, and Harrison, trying to fix them. Periodically they come to me asking if I'm okay. One Brit asks, 'hey mate you had any morphine yet?' Finally I accept because they have plenty and I know it doesn't need to be rationed for my teammates. We get to Camp Leatherneck and they land and take us in. The corpsmen are looking at me, and I'm motioning to them that I want a picture, a mirror because I don't know what my face looks like. I want to see what happened. They can't find a mirror, so they take a camera from one of my buddy's flak vests and they show it to me, and I was like, 'Holy shit!' But I'm happy because I'm alive and I'm half smiling in that picture; partially because I'm high on morphine but mostly because I'm just happy to be alive. I was being wheeled into surgery, and I'm high-fiving everyone on my way down the hallway because I am so happy. Then a nurse comes over to me and tells me I am going to feel a sharp pain in my neck and to count backward. I counted two seconds and I was out. When I woke up there was a cute Danish nurse giving me a sponge bath and I thought I might be in heaven. I fell in love; the sponge bath was the gentlest thing that had ever happened to me in my entire life.

They did what they could to me and all I wanted to know was how my buddies were. They all made it through but they still…"

Povas took another break at this point in the story. He was shivering uncontrollably on an unusually warm spring afternoon. Unsure of how to comfort him and ready to end the interview, I put my hand on his and asked if he wanted to stop. He looked up at me and the pain in his eyes was palpable. He said he wanted to continue – he took a deep breath in and returned to his story.

"Josh Sweeny, the guy who lost both legs, was still in critical condition. They couldn't move him until they had him stabilized. I don't remember many details; I was too drugged. I think they moved us out first. I got flown to a facial expert in Afghanistan and then to Germany.

In Germany, they started doing a bunch of tests on me. They asked me if I was okay, what happened, how my mental status was, how my hearing was. I just kept saying I was fine. I wanted back in the fight. I ended up here in San Diego and once I got here I started telling the doctors here that 'I'm fine'. I don't think anyone had any intention of sending me back. I go through the whole process, and surgeries and then the 3/4 returned from Afghanistan. I realized then that I wasn't going back to my unit anytime soon.

I totally denied any sort of emotional problems the whole time until I sat with Marla Knox one day. I was in her office, and she was asking me all kinds of questions while she was helping me prepare for a skiing trip. She asked too many questions and I started crying there in her office. She told me I needed to see a therapist and talk about the things I had held inside.

It sunk in that I wasn't going to be able to stay in the Marine Corps and do the only job I wanted to do (Scout Sniper), and I was medically retired in 2012. During that time, I moved to Freedom Station. It was more than a place to live. Sandy helped me smooth things out in my life; she helped me with the transition and helped

61

me get into school. I wanted to give back, so I started fixing things here and there. That turned into Sandy asking if I wanted to be the property manager and I took her up on the offer. I will stay here while I'm in school working on my Finance degree. My goal is to get my degree and go into medical sales. I'm comfortable here, and I'm thankful that I was able to come here through my transition time, and I'm still in transition. I will be for a while."

I thoroughly enjoyed my time getting to know Povas. He was a pleasure to interview and exceptionally articulate. To watch him fall apart in front of me during parts of the interview was an experience I will never forget. I don't know that I will ever get over watching the pain shown on his face, in his eyes or the way his body language changed to that of a small, scared child during parts of his story.

For Povas, Freedom Station has been a place of safety and healing. He is one of the front-men that Sandy relies on to keep an eye out for the others who reside there. It is often said that things happen for a reason and in some cases I believe that to be true. I know Sandy and Freedom Station have helped Povas significantly through his transition. But Povas has helped countless other wounded guys who have entered the gates of Freedom Station and I believe he was placed there for that reason.

CHAPTER 12

WHAT LEVEL ARE YOU?

The dull click-clack sound of metal hitting asphalt mixed with something mimicking that of a semi-violent struggle caused me to turn my head slightly in its direction. I noticed a black BMW had backed into a handicap parking space directly in front of the entrance to Freedom Station. I stood there to the right of the code secured entry gate moving nervously back and forth from one foot to the other while staring at the screen on my phone, hoping the director would return my call and let me inside the gates for our scheduled meeting. I watched him walk toward the gated entrance from behind the cover of my dark sunglasses, and I knew he had to be one of Freedom Station's warriors. He never looked in my direction focused on the seemingly difficult task at hand. Walking.

Beads of sweat covered his slick, bald, head and as Toran walked through the gate I could see the back of his shirt was wet with perspiration from the fifty-step workout he had just endured. Having the opportunity to keep my gaze on him from the back, I realized that I had no idea where I was or what Freedom Station was all about. I also realized I had just witnessed my first glimpse of what the human side of war looked like. Completely caught up in the moment I almost missed her call.

"Hello, dear. Are you here?" Sandy asked.

"Yes, I am right in front of the gate."

"Wonderful. I will send one of my guys down to let you in."

I stared down at the phone in my hand, praying it wouldn't be him that she sent. But, a few minutes later he reappeared, this time in a wheelchair. He stared at me as the gate opened, an angry expression on his face, and his broad shoulders slumped forward.

"Why didn't you tell me you were waiting to get in?" he asked in a sharp tone.

"I didn't want to bother you," I answered, feeling like an idiot as the words left my mouth.

"It was more of a bother to come back down here and let your ass in."

He turned his chair and quickly wheeled away. I felt like a jerk. I'm uncertain as to why I didn't tell him I was waiting to get in the gate. I still don't know. I felt an odd mixture of fear, embarrassment and nervousness. I didn't know what to say to him. I didn't want him to think I was staring at him – even though I was. Not wanting to treat him differently than I would anyone else, I feared that upon opening my mouth, I might do just that. So I had pretended he wasn't there. That was my first introduction to Toran Gaal.

By all accounts, Toran Gaal had a rough start in life. Adopted as an infant from India, he was brought to the United States before his first birthday and raised primarily by his adoptive grandparents. He grew up in a small town outside of Yosemite National Park in California. He had found his place in the world when he picked up a basketball for the first time as a youngster.

Toran was a natural athlete and grew from the malnourished infant into a 6'3" powerhouse. Putting in time on the court paid off big. At seventeen, he earned a full-ride scholarship to a Division I college. He left California in pursuit of his dream; however, it wasn't long before that dream, and his calling, changed. After his second college basketball season in early 2006, he followed in his older brother's footsteps and in a matter of days made the decision to leave college for the Marine Corps.

"I felt a duty to serve, honorably, the country that had saved my life. I wanted to leave my mark and make a difference," Toran said of his decision to join the Corps.

Toran chose the Marine Corps because he knew his brother, Dominic, would tease him if he chose any other branch. As most Marines will tell you, there is only one branch – The Marine Corps. He entered as an infantryman. His first unit was out of Camp Lejeune in North Carolina. Being sent to the East Coast didn't make the California kid happy but being in the Corps came with sacrifices – Toran understood that early on. After six short months in he deployed for a seven-month tour in Iraq. "It wasn't bad. We didn't take much fire," he recalls.

Soon after returning from Iraq, he was called to the White House for Presidential Guard Detail. A high honor for any Marine but for Toran it was way outside of his comfort zone. "There I was – coming from Iraq to a place where I had to be polished and in the spotlight. I didn't know how to do that. I hated White House detail. Meeting the President was a huge honor, but this wasn't why I joined the Corps."

He made a decision immediately after learning he would be spending time stateside. Education was important to him, and he chose to spend his off-duty time wisely by finishing his college courses and earning a BA in Business Administration from Georgetown University.

After six months at the White House Toran got what he wanted. "I got orders back to my original unit but they were looking for combat replacements for another unit. I jumped on that. I knew I would get to go back over there and that's what I wanted."

Toran deployed to Marjah, Afghanistan in 2009. His experience there was "totally different" than Iraq. After five months, he came back to the states.

In Toran's Words

"When I returned from (that) deployment, I only had seven months left in the Corps. I finally got orders for the West Coast at Camp Pendleton. I went to the 1st Battalion, 5th Marines.

They had just returned from Afghanistan, so they weren't going back and that was a bummer. Then something strange happened and we were going to deploy. I found out I would have to re-enlist if I wanted to go on the deployment. After dragging it out for a few weeks, I was able to extend for the duration of the upcoming deployment. I knew though that I was staying in before we left for that deployment.

We deployed in March of 2011 to Sangin, Afghanistan. On June 26, 2011, my life took a drastic turn. I don't remember much, but several people who were there have given me the story through their eyes. I remember submitting my paperwork to re-enlist the day before, requesting a lateral move to EOD. Infantry wasn't enough of a thrill for me anymore; I wanted something bigger. I knew if I was going to die in a war I wanted to die doing something big. Gunny Pate died the same day I was injured. He was EOD and was the one who had inspired me to want to make that change. He was the best.

We went on patrol to make a raid on a compound. To cut the distance and get there by dawn, we headed out at night which we didn't usually do because the IED threat was so high. We shacked up in an empty compound to get some sleep. Our sweeper cleared the area, and we settled in – setting up posts for some to hold watch while others slept. I was asleep on a ledge maybe three inches off the ground and rose at approximately four-fifty in the morning to wake up my guys. I remember waking up and stepping off of the ledge. I stepped directly on a twelve-pound pressure plate IED. My Marines told me they thought our compound got hit.

The blast propelled me into a metal wall that served as the door to the compound crushing the entire left side of my face. My skull was open exposing my brain, and my eye was out of its socket. My left leg was blown off completely above the knee, and my right leg was mangled, intact by only threads. I was the first casualty of the day; Gunny Pate was the last."

Toran paused and looked away from me for a moment. When he turned his face back toward me, I could see he had tears in his eyes. He straightened his posture, cleared his throat claiming to have something in his eye and continued his story.

"One of my junior Marine's took shrapnel in the head from the blast and we got medevaced together. The majority of what I know about the blast was told to me by others who were there. I don't have many of my own memories. My junior Marine said that he asked the British pilot if I was going to be okay and the pilot responded with his hands in the thumbs-up sign. He said looking at me though, he thought there was no way I would survive.

I was taken to Camp Bastion then Bagram. From there I went to Germany then Bethesda. Once at Bethesda my brother, Dominic, received my body and my grandparents arrived a day later. Dominic had to make all of the medical decisions on my behalf because I spent the first two and a half months in a coma. I had a severe infection in my right leg which resulted in five more amputations; eventually the last one took the rest of my leg and my hip. There wasn't a choice, it was my hip and the rest of my leg or my life; my brother made the right decision. I can't imagine what it must have been like for my family – having to make decisions that would change my life – to save my life. I remember waking up a few times. At first, I thought I had been captured; another time I thought I was still in high school and had been in a car accident. That time is hazy and I only have fragmented memories.

From Bethesda I was sent to Palo Alto to a polytrauma unit. When I arrived in Palo Alto, I was so angry at the world. I couldn't talk; I could barely hold a pen. All I remember is that I didn't want to be kicked out of the Marine Corps. I spent five months at Palo Alto. I did some physical therapy there, but the primary focuses were speech therapy, mental health, and vocational therapy. When I left Palo Alto, my next stop was San Diego. I still didn't get it, you know, I was still angry when I arrived in San Diego at Balboa. I thought everyone owed me something, and I didn't know how to communicate. I had to have a few more surgeries; the last one was to reverse my colostomy.

I was lucky enough to be matched with a great prosthetist, Randy Whiteside. He had no idea what he was going to do with me, but he just started trying different things and it worked so we ran with it. I started out on my stubbies – short legs basically to practice on. I started walking around the hospital a bit. After that last surgery, I had about a three-week gap before I could leave the hospital. I practiced a lot on my legs. I started walking on my legs, short distances; I couldn't walk that far because I don't have a hip, so it was hard to walk for very long and it was extremely frustrating. But having my legs made it so much easier and more comfortable to sit. It was a six-month process from my stubbies to getting around on my legs with knees. I also spent a lot of time in therapy. I have a hard time with communication and relationships. I think I will be in therapy for a long time.

Being at Balboa helped me a lot. Being around my Marines and other guys who have injuries; it just made me feel closer to the military being there. I felt like I had a purpose. I didn't want to let any junior Marines see me struggle and that pushed me to be better or get up on my knees sooner. I wanted my independence back – I didn't want to have to rely on anyone. I felt like I was still a leader. My amputations are not the worst of my injuries; it's my brain injury that makes life hard. I can figure out the walking part, but not being able to remember what day it is or what medications I'm supposed to take sucks. I was always outspoken, but now I don't know how to filter what I say and I end up hurting people's feelings even when I don't mean to.

The people at Balboa kept trying to push me to do other therapies like surfing. They tried really hard to get me to play wheelchair basketball, but I will never play basketball again. Never.

I started surfing, and then I did a marathon on my hand-cycle and I loved it. I also started going to CrossFit Del Mar. I have a cross-fit competition coming up soon and a series of marathons. I am getting ready to do four marathons in four weeks. Next year I'm thinking about riding across America on my hand-cycle. All of that helps me. It makes me feel like I am still doing something positive with my life. I want to inspire other people to continue to be active after injuries.

The first time I was introduced to Sandy and Warrior Foundation, she was at Balboa giving out backpacks for Christmas. I was angry about it because I didn't understand why they were giving this stuff to us, the injured guys, instead of to the guys at Pendleton who were still serving. It took me a long time to understand that there were organizations that wanted to help us. They wanted to make things easier and better for us. I had to take a step back and look at the big picture. I'm close to a lot of the volunteers at Warrior Foundation Freedom Station; they are my family here in San Diego.

I moved to Freedom Station in 2013. Being able to move into my place at Freedom Station was a new beginning for me. I had to learn how to do things for myself, and I needed that transition time. Being in the hospital, it's hard to learn how to do anything for yourself because people are doing almost everything for you."

Toran became quiet for a moment. When he began speaking again, his words were measured carefully, and I could see his emotional pain in his facial expressions.

"At my retirement, I spent a lot of time reflecting on what happened and all that was lost. Getting out was hard for me not only because I wanted to stay in, but also because I had lost guys who didn't have that choice anymore. Like Gunny Pate – I knew he would have stayed in. I felt like I should stay in, for him. I know he would want me to live my life for me, and it's hard to explain those feelings to someone who doesn't know what its like to lose a brother out there. Pate and the other guys I lost are always with me. I have them tattooed on my arm, and I know they would want me to live my life. The civilian population wants to honor us, the injured guys, and that's cool, but the guys who didn't come back and the guys who are still out there serving – that's who we should honor – that's who we should be thanking for their service.

I retired from the Marine Corps in February of 2014. I have done several internships and worked for Congressman Duncan Hunter. I have been able to prove to myself that I can live independently; I can drive myself where I need to go, and I enjoy the sports and physical activities I take part in. I can honestly say that the last eight years of my life have been the best eight years of my life. I've seen people overcome obstacles that didn't seem possible. People have seen me overcome things that didn't seem possible. But, at the end of the day, I regret getting out of the Marine Corps. Every day. I was a good leader, and think I could have made a career out of it. People tell me not to regret it, but I do. Getting out is my only regret."

⎯⎯⎯⎯◉⎯⎯⎯⎯

I was nervous when it had come time to interview Toran. I remember driving to meet him that evening like it was yesterday. When I arrived at his cottage, I was instantly aware of our connection – it was immediate, and it was powerful. This interview was much different than the others. I felt like I had known him my whole life. After a few minutes of idle chatter, I turned on my recorder, and we got started. Early into the interview he said something that will stay with me forever. It struck me like an arrow piercing my soul; it woke me up from the complacency I had adopted.

"I do this because some woman, somewhere, might pick up an article or a book and read this, and she might be at the end of her rope. Maybe she will read this and think her life isn't so bad. Maybe she will read this and know she can go on, too."

Maybe it was because he referenced a "woman" or maybe it was just what I needed to hear at the time. Maybe he referenced a woman because he was talking to me, and I am a woman – I don't know. What I do know is that I left with a different mindset than when I arrived. His story is undoubtedly an amazing one, but it was more than his story that affected me that evening. It was everything about him. It was everything about us. It was an awakening for me – one that I needed and at the very moment that I needed it most. It was a breath of fresh air. It was a kiss at the very core of my being. It was everything and nothing all at the same time. It was the most magical moment of my life. It changed me. He changed me. Knowing him changes me every day. And so began our journey.

The months that followed our interview are a blur. Toran and I began secretly dating. I had reservations because of the age difference, but I couldn't deny what my heart was telling me to do.

70

Becoming involved in a relationship with Toran opened my eyes to experiences that I would have never been able to understand fully or articulate but for being a part of them. It has been almost two years of many highs and lows. I've seen the physical and emotional struggle of Toran's 'after' with my own eyes – I've been a part of it. Hearing about such struggle and being a daily witness to that struggle allow for two altogether different perspectives. Being sucked into the world full of extreme uncertainty is similar to getting the wind knocked out of you multiple times a day. Almost as painful is the unbearable truth that this is your life – for the rest of your life. There is no way to fix it, change it or ignore it. I have come to understand that there is, however, a way to normalize the insanity of living with not only life changing physical injury, but also game-changing emotional trauma.

There is a danger, however, in over-normalizing this existence. If you are successful in normalizing the situation completely, it becomes easy to minimize the harsh reality. Toran and I have both done this, specifically in 2015, and we both paid the price. Eventually, we found ourselves taken by surprise on some random day, by some regular occurrence like no available handicap parking on a rainy day when he is wearing his legs and the closest open spot is a football field away. He gets upset because he wants to go into the store with me and I get upset because I don't want him to walk that far in the rain. It hits us like a ton of bricks and we snap back to our reality. It's important to learn to adapt and know that improvisation has to be a part of our lives. I feel better equipped today to recognize the line that we sometimes cross, together, and that line scares me. However, to find that 'normal' feeling I am frequently stepping ever closer to it. I suppose this paints the picture of our dance. Like everyone else – we make mistakes, fall, get back up and start again. My biggest fear is and will continue to be the what-ifs. What if he can't get back up next time? What if he, too, becomes a statistic? What if I fail him? I believe that is a worry for many of us – the caregivers and the wives of war. War isn't selective of its victims, and it doesn't mind sharing its devastation. War is far reaching, and its ripple effect can range far beyond the battlefield. It has taken almost two years for me to understand that but understanding doesn't make it easier.

Even with all the ugliness and struggle, I wouldn't change the journey or my eventual destination. Our house is regularly filled with laughter and smiles. Every day I see accomplishments big and small from Toran and the rest of the family from watching Toran successfully navigate an inaccessible home to my tiny little girl hefting a wheelchair in and out of the back of a pick-up truck. Hearing a little boy in an elementary school classroom inquire about Toran's rank by asking, "What level are you?" to my daughter matter-of-factly proclaiming, "I couldn't find your backpack so I just put the pencil in your leg." One of the greatest times to date was watching Toran get back on the basketball court. Never say never. He returned as a youth coach and the lessons he teaches his kids significantly exceed learning the game of basketball. There are hundreds of moments that I can't help but smile about when I replay them in my mind. A new normal, indeed.

The world can be a cruel place for someone like Toran. People stare, ask inappropriate questions and are just downright rude sometimes. They are often insensitive to the plight of daily life with severe and debilitating injuries. We have those who take out their anger over war and politics on those who served this great country, and that is something I will never understand. Some days I feel like we are at risk of becoming misanthropic, but then a kind soul will pop up out of nowhere and extend some small gesture that reminds me there is goodness all around us, and we have the wounded military community who help with healing and understanding.

A lot changed in my life following my interview with Toran, in fact, just about everything in my life changed. The more time I spend with him, the stronger our bond becomes. I knew he was my forever; I just didn't know how we would get there. The process by which that happened – is still happening – has been enlightening, frightening and challenging. Most of all, it has shown me a strength of the human spirit that I didn't know existed. It has shown me a side of myself that I didn't know I had, and it has shown me what real, true, raw love looks like, and how it feels. It's easy to be loving, happy and grateful when life is good and nothing is broken. To feel and express those emotions while daily life is a struggle – well, that is a feat that many are never able to pull off.

I consider myself unbelievably lucky to walk through his days with him. To see Toran at his best and his worst and to watch all of the in-between is a gift. For myself and those in my close circle to be able to witness what his daily life consists of and how beautifully he pulls it off is a gift that I wish more people could experience. Every day brings new experiences, and every morning I pinch myself – I can't believe this is my life. I can't believe I get to do this every day – I get to be in the presence of a man who shines such a bright light. It is surreal most days. I keep expecting to wake up and go through a regular day – a day of nothing particularly eventful – you know, just an average day. As far as I can tell there is no such thing as an average day with him. Every day is a crazy mix of adding to my gray hair and having my heart beat so fast and hard that I think it might burst. This is what love is supposed to be. How did I get to be the one? I ask myself this question, too. I have quit trying to answer it, though. I don't care why or how anymore; I am just thankful to be here.

CHAPTER 13

DOC SCHNEIDER

We often overlook the emotional scars that stay with those who treat the injured on the battlefield. I believe these unsung heroes are among the most affected when they return from war. I know one such warrior, Justin Schneider – 'Doc' to the guys. His quick thinking, professional application, and poise under pressure saved Toran's life. Although Doc doesn't like to take credit for his part in Toran's second chance at life, it is a fact that but for him Toran would not be with us today.

I am incredibly thankful that Justin is a part of Toran's life. When I watch the two of them interact I can't help but smile. I can't relate to the bond they have. I don't think many people can, but it is a beautiful interaction to witness. I am blessed to be able to see it with my own two eyes.

In Doc's Words

"I think back on the day of the IED blast that caused Toran's injuries. I remember the sights, the smells, and the actions everyone in the squad took to make sure we got Gaal out of there as quickly as possible. It wasn't until we put him on the helicopter that it truly sank in.

Gaal was a leader, and although sometimes the stuff he did or said got under my skin, we all respected him. Watching his recovery, accomplishing as much he has; it's inspirational. I've watched him adapt and overcome his physical challenges as well the mental, even though those injuries can be the hardest to heal. Being involved in his life since his accident and talking about that day and the events that took place after has helped in my mental recovery.

Every combat veteran who makes it home unscathed thinks back to the ones who didn't come home or the ones who came back physically different. We feel that it should have been us instead. I blamed myself for a few things and had some dark thoughts for a long time; I couldn't even talk to the Marines I had treated for injuries. The invisible wounds are the hardest, and I know that each one of us struggle to deal with that in our own way.

The friendship Toran and I have is different than most other friendships. He often thanks me for doing what I did, what we as a squad did to bring him home and that's when it all makes sense. We all had different reasons for being there doing what we were doing, but at the end of the day it was all about the guy to the left and right of you. The selflessness I witnessed during our deployment still amazes me and in some crazy way makes me wish I could go back, with the same guys, to do the same thing. Watching the gentlemen that I was with for those seven months overcome their injuries, start or add to their families, and live successful and happy lives has helped in my recovery.

I hope that all veterans know that when the days seem dark – even though you might not have remained in touch – they always have the guys that were next to them to talk to, to come to for support. Toran's story is one I tell often. The fact that he was able to overcome it all, pick himself up and get to where he is today is always a great story. From competing in marathons to riding across the country on a hand bike, his positive attitude while doing it inspires people. It proves that our wounded warriors are still here and still capable of doing great things."

CHAPTER 14

A NOTE FOR CAREGIVERS

Postwar life impacts more than the service members. Unfortunately, those of us who have the great honor, and at times self-appointed obligation, to care for combat-injured veterans do not have an extensive network of resources. Just like our husbands, wives, sons, daughters, sisters or brothers we are often on our own to make it all work out somehow. I find that fact as reprehensible as I find the lack of mental and emotional help our veterans receive from the Veterans Administration.

Caregivers, like our veterans, have stories of pain and sorrow. They often struggle with psychological and emotional trauma, broken relationships and guilt when all they do isn't enough to bring relief or bridge the gulf that war experiences have created between them and those they love.

I entered into the world of 'life after the war' when I began a relationship with a man who had seen three deployments and suffered a catastrophic injury that ended his last one early. I had no idea what living with him daily would be like. I went in with an open heart and the desire to nurture. What I discovered is that I can't banish his demons; I can only help him fight them. I can't erase his memories or the feelings associated with them. I can't make his physical challenges disappear either. That was an agonizing realization for me. To know that you can't make the person you love feel better leaves one feeling helpless.

I fell in love with Toran for many reasons. Our connection was immediate and made me feel in ways I had never experienced in any other relationship. One of the first things I noticed about Toran was his positive attitude and how he seemed to glide through life as if he hadn't a care in the world. I found his attitude puzzling given what I assumed he had seen and been through. It wasn't until I sat down to interview him that I learned the ugly truths; at the time I had no idea that he hadn't shared the ugliest of them all. After hearing his story, I fell even harder.

In the beginning, it wasn't all that challenging. Once Toran and I became serious, I started hearing from people who had been in his life long before I came into the picture. They told me how much he had changed and how happy he seemed – always crediting me with this miraculous transformation. I too witnessed him blossom into a more positive human being than he had been when we first met.

The outward change was nice, but inside, he felt the same terrible insecurity and guilt that had been there, waiting to come out and cause mass destruction. I saw small signs here and there but always chalked it up to 'one of those days.' We all have them. I granted him immunity convincing myself that he had it worse than anyone I knew and deserved to have his outbursts overlooked.

In the beginning, I will admit, it felt good to have others believe I was changing this man; the man I loved. That he was less angry, insecure and anxious because of me was a beautiful feeling but also a temporary one. Similar to the first time you open a tube of super glue, I learned that eventually my ability to piece him back together with any permanence was just as unlikely as opening that super glue tube for the fifth time expecting the thin stream of ultra-adhesive magic to seal forever a chasm. What I learned was that each day is about repairing and building further the bridge between our loved ones, irreparably changed, and the world they have returned to.

One evening Toran and I were at my home, and he was in a grumpy mood changing the usually light energy in my home into something thick and dark. I was frustrated and didn't understand how a lovely evening could go south so quickly and for no apparent reason. For the first time in our relationship I called him on his corrosive behavior. I wasn't soft or passive. My words were spoken to him while tears streamed down my face. I gave him the best advice I could think of at the time, and I gave it to him with a sharp tongue. I figured out that a huge part of his anger and depression came from losing guys over there, but it was something he rarely spoke of. I knew it had a dramatic effect on him because of observations I had made. The bracelet he always wore, the American flag hanging in his living room with names written on it followed by 'Never Forgotten' and the way a sad country song would put him in a trance and send him staring off into space. Bella, our daughter, and I have a term for that far-away stare; we call it 'glitching'.

"You are not honoring them by throwing your life away or ruining your relationships by pushing those that love you away. Do you want to honor them? Live your life. Remember them, but do not hold onto the past so hard that you let it destroy your present or your future." That's what I told Toran that night.

Toran had a full calendar the year we started dating. Between surf competitions and marathons, he spent most of his time at my house. We fell into a routine without ever discussing it. There was no discussion of personal preferences and routines let alone special needs. I thought I could figure out what needed to be modified for him, and he allowed me to believe that was the truth. He always used the spare bathroom, and I assumed it was because he was trying to respect my space in my master bathroom. I found out later it was because there was a stool in that bathroom that he used to get up to the toilet. I did all the cooking and cleaning in the kitchen; assuming again that he felt the kitchen was the woman's area – never did it occur to me that he couldn't reach anything in that kitchen. He would use my master bathroom to shower, and I found it odd that he would leave his toothbrush and razor in a cup on the floor of the shower. It was because he couldn't reach the bathroom sink.

As we spent more time together in a home environment, I began to understand Toran's limitations and we adjusted accordingly although rarely did we do it with grace. Typically the adjustments would take place after a blow up; he would become frustrated by my hovering and smothering and I with his grumpiness and what I felt was ungratefulness. It took us time to learn how to communicate our feelings. I came to understand that he hated asking me for help and felt like he wasn't doing what a 'man' should do and it was easier for him to do things the hard way, unsafe ways or go without rather than ask me for help. It took him time to understand that it hurt my feelings when I was trying to help and he snapped at me. It took him time to believe that my attempts to make things easier for him were not me insinuating that he wasn't capable. These are things we should have discussed long before they caused arguments between us, but how does one know how to bring up the topic of things you can or can't do around the house when you don't have legs? I can tell you who doesn't – the person without legs and the person who loves that person. It's awkward. It's not something you can walk into a bookstore and pick up a how-to manual for. Maybe someday I will write one of those – assuming I ever figure out the step-by-step guide to being a wife and caregiver for a combat-injured veteran.

The new year came and we took a trip to see Toran's family. He hadn't spent much time with them after his injury and when they were there during his hospitalization he was medicated and not the most coherent. I was on his butt regularly about reaching out to them. I questioned why he spoke so harshly to his grandpa and why he seldom picked up the phone to call his brother. It didn't seem normal. I speculated as to the reasons and told him I thought it was important for him to see his family. I never considered how going back home would feel for him. I didn't think about him seeing old pictures, places he had played basketball in his youth or the home he had walked out of the last time he was there. I figured I knew what I would want if he were my child. I thought about it from a parent's perspective instead of from his perspective. Meeting his family and being in a living room where he had spent his childhood, the uneasiness between he and his family was evident. While driving back home from that trip, it finally occurred to me how painful it must have been for him. Of course, I didn't say anything to him about my epiphany because how do you talk about understanding the emotional pain of such a life-altering injury with the man who is living in that pain?

At the end of that January, Toran and I got engaged and we realized we really had to figure out our living situation. He was living in transitional housing, and I was in a lease, so we agreed it made sense for him to move into my house. I cleaned out half of my closet to make space for his stuff – okay, a third of my closet – and a few drawers. One night I was lying in bed and asked him a question that had been on my mind for days. He had been bringing a new, full backpack with him every day. I asked a few times when he wanted to move his stuff in and he avoided the questions by saying he didn't have time. I asked him about the backpacks, and he got quiet for a few minutes. I pointed out the fact that the bottom of the closet was starting to pile up with full packs and inquired as to what was in them. He let out a long breath and told me why. He couldn't reach the rack in the closet, and he didn't want all his stuff in my way. He also let me know the reason he hadn't brought his prosthetic liners in from his trunk was because his 'special' stuff took up too much space. That broke my heart. To know that he thought his stuff was in my way and that I still had no clue how to accommodate his needs was a crushing blow. The next day I went out and got plastic drawers and stacked them three high in the bottom of the closet for him to put his clothes in although it seemed little consolation to offer for my oversight.

I imagine that the continuous fumbling through our new life is the natural, albeit strange, rhythm for anyone in our position. That's easy for me to say now; back then I thought it was a hopeless puzzle that we would never figure out. I had no idea who to ask for advice or where to turn for help. I didn't have any girlfriends who could relate, and I spent a lot of time buried in work to avoid dealing with it.

February came, and another funeral came with it. This funeral hit Toran hard; it was for one of *his* Marines. I knew many of the people in attendance, and it took everything I had not to fall apart watching the amount of pain felt by all. After the funeral Toran withdrew again and I could see him slipping into a dark place. I asked him to reach out to one of his mentors and one of my favorite people in the world, Jack Lyon. Toran spent a few hours on the phone sitting in his wheelchair, in the middle of the street in front of our house talking with Jack. I could hear his yelling all the way in the living room. I peeked out through the blinds and watched him for a moment; he appeared broken, defeated and scared. I had no idea what to do – there was nothing I could do. When he finally came back to the house, we both acted like everything was fine even though we both knew that was a lie. I learned later that Toran's angst after that incident was the worry that if it could happen to that Marine, it could happen to him too. Suicide. It is the specter that haunts even the strongest of our veterans.

It's easy to spout statistics. The media takes a line and runs with it and pretty soon the tag-line is on the tip of everyone's tongue. '22 A Day'. Yeah, I know you've heard it. It isn't entirely accurate, but we can leave that point for someone else to debate. What is true – painfully true – is that it happens, and it happens with unprecedented frequency within the combat veteran community. Why? There are some theories out there, and there is a massive amount of speculation. I believe the likelihood of it happening increases exponentially for those who do not have a strong support network around them and people paying close attention. I also think that sometimes no matter what measures are in place, for some the thought of being free from emotional pain far exceeds the will to go on another day. I don't know what the answer is. I wish I had a solution or alternative to offer but there isn't one. The pain is going to be there; the challenge is learning how to not only deal with it but to thrive in spite of its existence. I know with Toran the best days he has are days when he has exciting things going on, things that make him excited about living. That could be a new garden tool, pumping up basketballs or riding across America. It doesn't have to be something significant or particularly special. You just have to be able to recognize the beauty in simplistic everyday occurrences – the ones you would miss if you were gone.

Continually seeing the '22 A Day' statistic in the media affects us, the caregivers, also. In addition to worrying about the myriad of daily physical challenges that our veterans face, we are ever reminded that assisting with the physical challenges is only part of our duty as caregivers. We must also be vigilant about identifying triggers that cause our veterans stress and signs that they are struggling emotionally. Nobody can explain what exactly those are, and I'm sure it varies depending on their individual experiences. We are left to figure it out, and that's scary. For me, that responsibility feels heavier by far most days than the responsibility of making sure Toran doesn't fall or glitch while operating a vehicle. I also feel constant worry about his emotional wellbeing. Most of the time I have no idea what to say or do to bring him back to this reality – our lives in the here and now. To know that I might miss a sign or not realize he has fallen into a depression until it's too late keeps me awake at night and causes me anxiety. Some days there is a lot of silence in our home, silence and walking on eggshells. I wish someone could tell me how to fix that too.

Toran had an exceptionally tough time in the fall of 2015. He admits to me now that he was suicidal; I knew he was at the time and did everything I knew to do in that situation. I reached out to his personal network of men who understood what he was going through and pointed him in the direction of the VA's crisis line. We began the task of getting him into a serious therapy program in August, and his first appointment was the following January.

During that time I was battling anxiety and it got to the point where it was unmanageable. Reaching out for help wasn't easy. I was the one who was supposed to be keeping it all together, keeping both of us afloat, and I was sinking. I asked my VA Caregiver representative for guidance and was advised to go to the VA for therapy. I attempted to make an appointment and was fairly shocked that I got a date only three weeks out. I hung on as best I could. On the day of my appointment, I was told that there was an error in scheduling and that I would have to return the following week. By then I was having panic attacks, and I was scared that would happen in front of Toran. The last thing I wanted to do was let him see me fall apart. I reached out to Tricare and told them the situation and was given several doctors names. I must have dialed ten doctors that day. The soonest appointment I could get was a month out. I ended up going to urgent care just to get anxiety medication. I returned to the VA for my re-scheduled appointment and am so thankful it was I sitting in that chair and not a suicidal veteran.

My appointment was with an intake coordinator. She took me into a small office and began asking me standard questions about my age, family structure, physical health and the like. During those questions, her personal cellular phone was on the desk. She replied to multiple text messages and took one phone call. Then she moved on to extremely personal questions and at the tail end of a breath-stealing question, just as I was about to answer, she answered her personal cellular phone again. I left shortly thereafter and was beside myself with anger and disgust. I thought about it for days, weeks and it made me sick to my stomach. I told my VA Caregiver representative about it, and his advice was for me to file a complaint. It still angers me when I think about it. If that was my husband and he was at the end of his rope, that incident may have pushed him over the edge – he or any other person going in to seek help. If it hadn't happened to me, I might not have believed it possible but it did happen and since then I pay closer attention when people talk about negative experiences at the VA. There is one thing that is undeniable; the VA system is broken. Until the VA identifies the shortcomings in psychiatric care and therapy for veterans and implements a practical solution, veterans seeking that care from the VA will continue to die. And until more caregiver resources and training are available, we will continue to fear the worst instead of being prepared and equipped to be a part of the solution.

Toran and I have lived together for over a year, and we are making it work. It's not all bad. There is an incredibly abundant amount of beauty in our relationship. We both put forth the effort to learn from each other, understand each other's needs better and grow. I believe most people looking in from the outside only see the fantastic stuff. They see him ride his bike across America wearing a smile in all the pictures. They didn't see all the tears, strife, physical exhaustion and the emotional toll it took on him – on all of us. People see him walking on his legs and say 'man, you are incredible.' They didn't see him wincing as he was first standing in them or almost fall five times before making it to his truck. They didn't see the two minutes it took him to get into his truck. They don't see me cry at night when he has a bad day or our daughter go to school worried because he is visibly in pain. I wish the world could see what we see; I wish the world could look through a caregiver's eyes. I wish every American could see the other side of war and understand that this sentence is forever. There's an expression 'you can't un-ring the bell.' Never was there a truer analogy than that when speaking of the experiences of war. It can't be undone. His mind isn't going to wake up one day and not remember, and his legs aren't going to grow back.

For the caregivers, I wish we could take it easy on ourselves. I wish we could worry less and smile more. I wish we could band together and come up with solutions that will help to heal our veterans and our families. The veterans – they stick together – once a brother, always a brother. I believe us caregivers need to do the same.

In a world full of bad news with negative rhetoric coming from every possible media outlet and evil spewing from every crack – vow to be one of the crazy ones. Be a person crazy enough to think that you, one single person, can do something to change the world. You can. We all can. And we should. That one good thing – the light you shine in the world – has the power to cause a ripple effect, and there is no telling how far and wide it might travel.

CHAPTER 15

THE BASKETBALL STAR

—————)(())(—————

Josue Barron joined a gang at age fourteen and walked that road through high school. He found acceptance from the older men who became mentors and father-figures to him. After high school, he found himself getting into trouble and came to a point where he felt he was being selfish and causing his mother undue stress. He received a ticket for graffiti and his mom had to pay the penalty. This became a turning point, and he began seeking an alternative to the life he was living and where he feared it would ultimately lead him.

One of Josue's friends told him about the Marine Corps. Where he grew up, there wasn't a large population of military service members or veterans in the area. Being a first generation American and having no family members who had served, he thought there was only an 'Army'. He hadn't even known it was an option. The Corps offered him a way out. He joined in 2007, at age eighteen, to get away from gang life. He wanted an opportunity to improve his life and learn skills that would help him make a difference.

Josue met and fell in love his wife, Debbie, after returning from his first deployment and they married less than a year after their first date. He attributes a large part of his recovery and rehabilitation to his wife's unwavering love and support and the opportunity at a second chance.

In Josue's Words

"I deployed to Afghanistan with the 3/5. We left in September 2010. That first month we had so many casualties. I had a feeling something was going to happen because so many people were getting injured; there were so many IEDs out there. The week before I was injured my best friend got hurt. He and his squad leader stepped on an IED; his squad leader died, and he lost his arms. We were close, we were friends, and I just felt something was about to happen. A week later, on October 28, 2010, me and another guy stepped on an IED and got hurt. From the moment I got injured, I couldn't see anymore because I took shrapnel to the face. I could hear what was going on during the time I stepped on it and when the guys were helping me and putting tourniquets on. I ended up losing my leg and my eye.

I was sent to Germany, but I don't even remember going through there. Then I went to Bethesda in Maryland. My wife was there before I arrived. When I woke up, I still couldn't see. I remember asking for my wife; that was all I wanted. I wasn't worried about missing a leg; I was worried about why I couldn't see. I wanted to know if I would regain my sight and the doctors told me we would have to wait. My eyes were swollen and bulged out, so we had to wait until the swelling went down. One eye went back to normal, but I still couldn't see anything out of it. My wife had to put eye drops in every two hours for a month. Eventually, I started seeing light in one eye, and it got better over time. The better it got, the more excited I was. After a few months, I got to where I was 20/20 with glasses in one eye, and I was happy about that.

From the time I woke up in Maryland, I was only worried about my sight. I accepted the fact that I had lost my leg – it wasn't a huge concern because I had bigger things to be concerned with. When I had my amputation, I wasn't that concerned. Once my vision got to the point where it wasn't going to get any better I had time to focus on other things.

I arrived at Balboa Naval Medical Center, and when you first get injured, they send in other amputees further along in the process to help motivate you. This Sergeant Major came out to see me and was telling me I would be all right – "look at me," he said, "you can do this." But my amputation was different than his. He had all this muscle left that I didn't have. That was hard for a while, but then I started meeting guys who had amputations to the hip and that kind of put it into perspective for me. I was thinking 'how can I complain' and I got motivated. I couldn't complain, I had a few inches to work with, and I could wear a socket for a few hours and be okay. I got to the point where I was just happy to be alive and happy to help motivate other people.

During my recovery at Balboa I had Marla Knox as a therapist and she was the right therapist for me. One day, about six months into my recovery, she asked what I thought about playing wheelchair basketball. I thought it was a joke; how do you play basketball in a chair? I had played street ball growing up but had never played on a team. I started playing with other guys from Balboa, and I was pretty good. I was able to start going to basketball camps with guys that had been playing in a chair for years. After attending a camp at the University of Illinois, I got hungry, and the competitive side of me came out. I wanted to be as good as the guys we watched play. I had no idea there was a whole world of disabled sports out there. I feel like my leadership skills grew while playing basketball. There were guys that didn't know how to play, so we all started learning together. That's when I felt my leadership skills come out; we were all learning, and I wanted to help the other guys. Wheelchair basketball also helped me gain my confidence back and made me want to be a leader.

In 2011, I met Sandy Lehmkuhler at a shooting range, and she gave me a pamphlet about Freedom Station. At the time Debbie and I were living in base housing at Point Loma and it was expensive. It was also a two bedroom and we didn't need all the space, it was just Debbie and I. At that time there weren't any couples or dogs living at Freedom Station, but I took a chance and went down to talk to Sandy. I asked her if Debbie and I could move in and let her know we had a dog. When I was going through the time of not being able to see, Debbie got the dog for me, a Yorkie. I never imagined myself with a small dog but for a while when I didn't want to go out in the world, that dog and Debbie were my only friends. I couldn't get rid of my dog. Luckily, Sandy agreed to take all three of us in.

When we moved into Freedom Station there were a few guys already there: Gunny Cano, Povas, and Spivey were there. After I had moved in, I started spreading the word around to other guys in my unit, and two of them moved in too. The whole place was filled with guys from Camp Pendleton. It was cool to be around the other guys, and it was so close to the hospital. Before we moved in, I was commuting from Point Loma to Balboa to go to all my appointments plus it wasn't like I could talk to my neighbors when we lived at Point Loma. I felt comfortable at Freedom Station because we all had something in common. I could sit on my porch and talk to other guys who could relate to what I was going through. There is a Starbucks nearby and at first I didn't want to go because I didn't want to go out in my wheelchair. But I did start going; I would go with another amputee who was also in a chair, and it was more comfortable going out with someone else like me. Then it wouldn't be people just staring at me – I wasn't alone – and that helped me have the confidence to go out in the world, around other people.

The beginning of my rehab I think was hard for my wife. She was only twenty years old and in a matter of fewer than two years our whole lives had changed. She had to drive me everywhere because I couldn't see. And, it wasn't that she didn't want to drive me, but it was a lot of time spent driving me to all my appointments. One day, I knew my wife was tired, and I just got in the car and drove, I drove myself. After that day I started driving regularly, and I gained a lot of independence. A lot of my buddies who got hurt had their wives leave them because it was too much stress; I felt very fortunate because Debbie stayed and we got through it together. It made us stronger.

I try not to complain. I got a second chance and there are guys from my unit who didn't – they didn't come home. When I started feeling down or depressed, I would remind myself of that. Like what do I have to complain about – I'm still here. I kept it all to myself. I didn't want anyone to know what I felt when I would get down. Keeping it to myself was easier for me; I didn't want anyone to know what I was going through on the inside. I also think to stay positive in front of my family, especially my mom helped to keep their spirits up too.

I help my family a lot, so for my mom and my siblings to see that I was going to be okay was a huge thing for them. I had changed physically, but I am still the same person. I am still able to contribute to my family and help them. I can help more now because I have retirement and my house is paid off. Now I can help them more than I was able to before. You can't forget about the struggle. You can't forget about where you came from and the people who helped you along the way.

Making the decision to get out of the Marine Corps was a hard decision, and I made it at the time because I was picky about the shoes I wore on my prosthetics. I didn't want to be in cammies with tennis shoes on, and I was new in my prosthetic and wearing boots didn't work for me. I also didn't want to sit behind a desk. During that time I also needed time to myself to figure things out; what worked for me, and what didn't. I still had issues and was still trying to figure out what I was capable of doing. I needed the last three years to myself; to play sports and just rebuild myself. I am at the point where I am ready to work; I'm comfortable with who I am and what I can do now. There are a lot of things I want to do, but I am going to focus on education first. I've thought of becoming a parole officer or getting a career helping teenagers in LA going through what I went through with gangs. At the same time, I get frustrated because I have a lot of family in LA still in the struggle, and I need to make money in a career so I can buy my mom a house and help my family. I am trying to decide what to do now.

My wife wanted kids, and I wasn't quite ready. We tried for two years, but I think we were both too stressed out during that time. We went to the doctor to make sure everything was working fine, and it was; it wasn't the right time I guess. Debbie and I were able to go to Paris for a week, and we decided during that trip to put the stress behind us. We found out she was pregnant right after that trip. I'm excited now. I think about all the times I was stressed, and I think about the guys that didn't come home. After you see guys not return home, it changes you. It makes you appreciate life. I try to remember what I have and always be thankful for what I have.

It's important not to hold too tight onto the past; you have to find another purpose. I think that's what messes a lot of guys up – they hold on to the past. A lot of guys also lean on drugs and alcohol and spend their time getting shit-faced – I want to spend my time working hard. I want to honor my friends and do something with my life because I still have my life. Too many take the easy way – I say challenge yourself. Be something you might not have been, do something good to help others and quit doing things to harm yourself. That isn't honoring the guys who died over there."

Since the time of our initial interview, Josue's family has grown. He and his wife Debbie now have two beautiful babies. I fully expect to see great things from Josue. His motivation and drive along with his strong desire to help disadvantaged youth will undoubtedly propel him into an arena where he will make a positive impact.

CHAPTER 16

SECRET SQUIRREL

———◦《◉》◦———

B rian Riley was born in Texas and raised in Wisconsin. Being the youngest of three, he was extremely close to his older sisters; one of whom he shares a birthday with – they were born two years apart on the same day. He competed in track and football during high school, but his love of writing led him to aspirations of being an author.

Generosity is something he grew up on, so helping others is a part of who he is. During the majority of his young life he practiced Tang Soo Do, eventually becoming an instructor to younger children. He credits the time he spent practicing martial arts with preparing him for the Marine Corps.

When his oldest sister joined the Marine Corps, he decided to follow in her footsteps, but he wouldn't join right out of high school. After high school, Brian began working as a roofer and enjoyed the physical challenge of that field of work. After a few years of working Brian decided it was time to join and in 2008, at age twenty-two, he went in on a Recon contract. One of Brian's regrets is that he is not always a better communicator and didn't tell people that were special to him how much he appreciated them, including his martial arts instructor, before he left.

In Brian's Words

"One of the strangest moments I had in the military was during a training exercise in Okinawa. There's a training area we frequently use. I'd gather people's routes, and they'd always go on the right side of this road. No one ever went to the left side. I wanted to find out what was over there. It was terrible. There's an excellent reason no one ever went over there. It was a triple canopy jungle, so we couldn't get a radio signal inside of it. We also didn't know what was underneath it because we couldn't get imagery or anything. It was up and down and all around. It was all like steep drops and then trying to go up incredible inclines, and it was miserable. We had to use ropes to scale some of the sections that we had to go up. I was in a draw and was the point man. I was looking at the leaves, and the sun was shining through them so they looked like emeralds. I thought to myself this is where I'm meant to be, right here. It was one of those weird moments because I had a ninety-pound pack on, my feet were soaked, and I was bleeding through my boots. We were going to have to start scaling our way back up, and all I could think was, 'It was meant to be.' I don't think I could ever explain that to someone unless they were in the middle of something miserable and they realized they'd rather be nowhere else.

BRC (Basic Reconnaissance Course) is where the Marine Corps started to feel like the Marine Corps to me. I smiled my entire way through. I was in the middle of the pack as far as physical performance went. I was the worst swimmer in my class. Not the worst per se, but probably about the worst you could be while still passing. I was so terrible at it. When I was going through recon and was walking up to the training door going into the compound, I'm like, 'Amphibious Reconnaissance huh? Amphibious, ain't that some shit?' I knew it was the part that I was going to have the most difficult time with. That was my flaw the entire time, up until we got fins. With fins, you can keep going and going and going. I felt sorry for my partner because I was so weak in the pool, but as soon as you put the fins on me, I could go forever because I didn't know how to quit.

I think BRC was also when I started getting a feel for the camaraderie of the Marine Corps. It wasn't a huge squad where you'd have eighty people in a bay. Each team had their little section, and I got to spend a lot of time with the people in my team.

I joined the Marines so that I could be recon. I knew I wanted to deploy as the point man of a recon team. One of the reasons why I wanted to be the point man and why I never swayed from that decision is because I figured I would be the most likely person to be able to handle the responsibilities and the inherent danger of that position. I wanted to be the point man because I figured I would have the best chance of getting through it. I had had two years to come to terms with the fact that I was probably going to be a double or triple amputee. That's one of the reasons why I don't have as big an issue with my injury because a single, below the knee amputee injury is easy-peasy. That kind of thinking is also one of the reasons why I wanted to go to Afghanistan because I also figured that as the first person at a scene, I would trust my judgment. A lot of that came from how much I started to understand the differences between Afghanistan and the United States. I was reading the articles and seeing that women could be beaten, stoned or killed for going to school. I was in Baltimore for a little bit before being deployed. We went out to bars and seeing the things that the women were able to wear and the things they were able to do – I realized that wasn't something they had in Afghanistan. Saying I was offended by that might be too strong but I knew that I at least wanted to do something, even if it didn't work out in the end. I wanted to do something so that they could get the same opportunities in Afghanistan as we had here in the states.

I've read a lot of books and one of the things I came across in a book I read stuck with me. One of the characters, her world view was she would rather think the best of someone and be wrong than believe the worst in them and be right. That's pretty much how I've always been. I didn't realize it until I read that part because I've always enjoyed giving people trust, especially if I think that they're in a position where they need it the most. There are a lot of people that, once they've developed a reputation, they can never get someone else to trust them. It seems like a vicious cycle. Often a person is going to become how you view them. I wanted to be the person that would always offer another a chance to prove themselves not only to me but themselves – that they can keep their word even if it's just something like being back in 10 minutes instead of an hour. Little goals.

When I got to Afghanistan, I knew the history of the area and what they had to deal with. I knew that it wasn't going to be easy. I did become disappointed in humanity, but I also got to see some of the beauty of humanity. On one of the patrols we were on, there was a farmer that we had developed a pretty good rapport with. We were on patrol around noon, and the heat gets sweltering over there. The farmer came out and gave us grapes. He wasn't asking for money or anything, he was giving us grapes out of generosity. That's something that if it were witnessed, it could have had terrible repercussions for him. Those grapes were his livelihood. He put his life on the line just so that he could share with us.

The children, probably the little girls, were the best part of the deployment. They're like a breath of fresh air. It was the little girls that held onto hope for change. The little boys, once they got much older than eight, the boys, they were trouble. It took us a couple of times to figure that out because we were going over there and we were supposed to win the hearts and minds and everyone. The first time we got swarmed by kids we were shaking hands, we were talk-ing, joking and whatnot. I was a point man at the time, so I was supposed to be holding the front security. I was getting a little bit nervous because these kids would be in front of me. If someone starts shooting at us, I would have to worry about kids being in the way of the combat which, it wouldn't have even been a question of whether I'd put their safety above mine. I would get them out of the way of fire. It was another complication that I would have to worry about. They also stole a lot of stuff from us. They took most of my map pens which were what we used to chart our routes and everything. There's so many of them; they would just get into our stuff. I think one of our guys got his watch stolen. Some of us were even giving pens out because we figured the pens maybe would help them with school. It wasn't until later that we found out that pens were starting to be used as detonators. That was an eye-opening experience.

It's a different world over there and not what I expected. I would do it again. I wouldn't make any changes. Maybe I would do it better, if I could. If I had to go through a whole Groundhog Day, even if no matter what I did it ended up with me with a traumatic injury, I would do it. I would willingly take that loop until I could get the best course for the people in that area.

I was in Sangin – vacation capital of the world. Despite what people tell you, I don't think we were ever winning in Sangin. Recon, I guess we did all right. We set a precedent that if you messed with us, we were going to push back hard, but we were also fair. You'll sometimes hear stories of guys that'd mess with the local nationals, but as far as I know, we never did that. We didn't want to ruffle feathers and make it even harder for ourselves. We got shot at a lot. It's weird because sometimes they would just shoot at us out of boredom like it wouldn't even be an insurgent or anything like that. It would just be a guy that has a gun and pops off a couple of shots.

I can never actually remember the day of my injury because oddly enough, it's never been crucial to me. My leg was amputated August 5 of 2011. The injury itself was sometime in July. Even before my actual deployment I sat down with my parents. I told them that I was deploying and when I was going through SOI, I had learned that the causality rate for my position was 90%, the people that were in the area before us – their injuries were double and triple amputees. When I was done with this deployment, chances were, I might be two limbs down or three limbs down. Honestly, the chance of me dying was more likely than me getting out unscathed. That was the conversation that I had with them before my deployment. They didn't break down in front of me. As it is, it probably wasn't exactly what they were expecting, but then again, I also had a lot more realistic view of my chances than other people do. I think one of the reasons why a lot of people have PTSD is because they go into a deployment and expect to be Superman. They don't expect anything bad to happen. I told a lot of jokes during our workup because, almost every training mission we did, I would go down as causality.

It was the last patrol that day before we were going to head back towards FOB Alcatraz. That seems to happen a lot. That's going to tell you how much we loved our FOB and how far out in the boonies it was. It was called FOB Alcatraz. We joked because none of us liked Okinawa, and we always called Okinawa Okatraz just because we were stuck there. It was our rock. We went from Okatraz to Alcatraz.

By that time, I had become unphased at getting shot at. The fact that the shot hit me lets you know how complacent I had become, but I got to be honest. The guy who was shooting at me was a good shot. His first rounds landed ten to fifteen feet from me. I kid you not; I had this moment where I paused mid-step and thought, 'You know, those were pretty close together.' I was astonished, almost pleasantly surprised. 'These guys aren't a waste of space. This guy knows what he's doing.' If you're going to be shot at, at least, there's a point of pride at being shot at by a professional. I was looking at the impact zone, like, 'Oh, no. I should be doing something more important right now.' I was along side of a wall, so there wasn't anything for me to drop behind, you drop down to the ground so that you make a smaller target for yourself, but I wasn't doing that. That moment, I was looking at the rounds, like, 'Oh, hey. If I look at how the dirt's curling I can tell where the impacts are coming from.' I knew the second rounds were going to be coming, and I braced myself to start running. The dude that was behind me slammed into me, and then I heard the second rounds of impacts and everything goes dark real quick. I wake up hitting the ground, and I hear people calling my name. My buddy, who had been holding security position ten meters in front of where I'd been shot, he was calling my name.

I was disoriented at that time. I wasn't going to try to respond by firing or anything like that, I just got up and ran to cover and hopped behind a wall. I remember seeing a guy and his son; they were alongside the wall as well. We were chilling out, just relaxing. The kid might have been freaking out; I might not have noticed it considering I'd just gotten shot, but he didn't appear to be as concerned as the adults. He was standing against the wall, looking down at me, and I was looking over at him. That's a normal day for him.

My buddy got a tourniquet on me. The shot hit about three inches above my ankle. It took out the tibia and fibula, shattered them, and took out the nerve cluster that wraps around one of them. That's probably why I blacked out for a moment; shock. There was one artery and skin holding my foot on. I didn't know how bad it was. I had gotten up and ran to cover. I didn't have any basis for how badly I was injured either. I got a feel for it when one of my friends ran over to the sandbags where I had flopped down behind to get me back inside the compound that we had just left. His response as he was turning the corner was, "Holy fuck!"

My biggest priority was not to make any sounds. I might not have fallen into the whole alpha personality, but I still had pride. We had been in engagements before, one of the insurgents was hit and we had heard him screaming and screaming and screaming. I wasn't going to let that happen. I didn't make a sound. As far as I know, I never made a sound. From what other people tell me and from one of my friends afterward when I met up with him, after my rehab, he was saying, "Yeah," He was saying, "Yeah. That was kind of a life changing moment. I decided if I was ever going to get hurt in the military, I was going to take it like you did."

They waited until the sun went down before they extracted me. The guys say I was talking about some science fiction stuff. I was really out of it when they got me out of the firefight. I was dealing with some British nurses. They're asking me for my Social Security number so they could put me in the system, but I had no idea what it was. I was still out of it. I had morphine in me. They were asking, "What's your Social Security number?" I'm like, "Really? That's what you want to ask me? Really?" They're like, "Don't worry. We're only going to buy a house in Mexico. You don't need to be concerned about it." I'm like, "Fine. You can buy a house in Mexico. I just have to come with you." So yeah, I eventually gave it to them.

They got me into Bastion. They thought I was going to keep my leg because I'd been shot and my leg was still attached which is better than what happens to a lot of guys that get blown up. All the doctors and nurses were telling me I'd be up and walking, and everything was going to be all right. I'd look down at my leg, and it had that metal cage on it to keep all the bones in place. It was an odd sight. While I was in that position, every once in a while, I would look down at my leg, and think, 'Oh, lefty, you're still there. Oh, righty! You're still there. Great.' I had an easy time of it because I was expecting something much worse.

One of the things that stuck out in my mind is a nurse. Nurse Emily. She was the first person I talked to when I was coherent. I have a deep and abiding affection for her because she was probably exactly what I needed at the time, kind and soft-spoken. I can still remember what she looks like. I know, probably for the rest of my life, I'm going to have a deep and abiding affection for her. A lot of the little kindnesses started to mean a lot more. When I got moved to Germany, there were two women handing out these little kiss stickers; I've kept it with me this entire time because it was one of the first little acts of kindness I got after my injury. It's something that I decided I wasn't going to throw away.

When I arrived at Balboa Naval Medical Center in San Diego, there were people handing out gift bags. It's little things like that that make me feel badly about how terrible I am with social situations because a lot of people don't understand how meaningful their actions can be. That's one of the things I have a hard time conveying to everyone. There's a lot of people I've come across before the military, during, and after that I'm never going to be able to convey how much they mean to me and how much of an impact they've had on me just because I'm probably not going to realize that I need to voice it until afterwards – until they're no longer part of my life.

For a long time, I thought I was going to keep my leg. Then, they finally set me up with a doctor. He started doing x-rays and assessing the damage. What finally made me decide that I had to have an amputation was the fact that I only had one artery going to my foot. Even if they fused my ankle and they managed to get rods in, my ankle wouldn't work right. It wouldn't be any different from the prosthetic ankle I have now. After a plethora of tests, x-rays and exams I finally agreed to the amputation. I woke up in so much pain after they took off my leg because I guess the block they put into me had come undone or because I moved. I had a lot of bad experiences with pain – phantom pain. I probably don't get it as often as a lot of people but generally, if I'm getting phantom pain, it feels like I've stepped on a nail or someone's pulling my toenails off. It's only been painful enough to take me down to my knees once, but there are plenty of times when I pause midstride and have to take a deep breath before I can take my next step. I had an easier time than other single below the knee leg guys because mine was a gunshot. I didn't have the secondary fragments that people who stepped on IEDs get. Having a knee makes a huge difference. I don't even know how I compare to other people. It took me three days to be able to walk unassisted.

I got involved with a lot of activities. I started doing some diving and Paralympic shooting packages. I moved into Freedom Station from Balboa. Once I was living on my own, I had time to reflect on the direction of my life. I had to do a lot of re-prioritizing. One of the things I realized is that I could do a lot more for the world with an engineering degree than by teaching people how to clear a room. It took me a while to figure that out because when I was going to rehab, there's a little bit of time thinking that, 'You know, how cool would it be to have a reconnaissance instructor who's a leg amputee but still keeping up with all these events and rough runs and everything like that? How motivating would that be for these guys?' For a while, that's what I was thinking – that I could get back into it. I got sick of the military, especially while I was in the hospital. So many of the guys, they weren't going to stay in the military because it just wouldn't be feasible for them. But there were still people on the chain of command that just loved hammering it in. Yes, you're still a Marine, but you aren't staying in the military – you're getting out – so cut the speech. That was one of many reasons why my time at Balboa got me to realize that I needed to get out of the military, out of the Marine Corps, do something with my life.

One of the reasons why I want to be an engineer is because I learned of an organization called Engineers without Borders. I'm assuming it's similar to Doctors without Borders. I would like to help build up underdeveloped countries. If sending in a military presence isn't helping them, maybe sending in a presence of infrastructure, something to build, to help them set up a bare foundation. Maybe that will help.

The most meaningful thing that Freedom Station did for me was to allow me my privacy because I'm learning how important my privacy has been to me. During my recovery phase, I didn't even know how it would affect me from a mental standpoint if I didn't have a place where I could relax, get away from it all and be unsupervised. I got to Freedom Station, and I locked my door. I could turn off all the lights. I could take a nap, get away from it all when I needed to or go out to do all the other activities that were available. I think my first six months at Freedom Station I spent two weeks out of every month out of state and out of the country. Just being able to come back and decompress, for those two weeks, that was huge for me. Freedom Station would do very well if it was multiplied or done again in other cities because there are more people who need it than just injured vets – there's homeless vets who could use a way to get back into the real world, get their footing back, get a nice base and then move on with their lives. I think this could be a huge benefit for a lot of people."

Brian Riley is still living at Freedom Station, focusing on school and physical activities. He is in the process of deciding where he would like to live long term. Although San Diego is beautiful, he says that he misses the snow and the change of seasons in Wisconsin. Brian's attitude about his injury was fascinating to me. He was extremely matter-of-fact and seems genuinely at ease with the loss of his leg. I believe his drive to further his education with the goal of improving the lives of others will benefit many.

CHAPTER 17

GUNNY

For Gunnery Sergeant, Juan Cano, telling his story isn't easy. He admits to falling into bouts of depression when he talks about his time in service and shies away from situations that put him in the position of telling his story.

When I began interviewing the men of Freedom Station, they would speak of other guys who had gone through the transition in the cottages, but no name came up more frequently than Gunny's. After hearing his story, I now realize that he was the first "warrior" to reside there. Even before Freedom Station was an actual transitional facility, Gunny lived in one of its units.

Being older than the typical Freedom Station resident, Gunny has invaluable insight that he openly shares with the younger men. He has become something of a mentor to many and says his ability to give back is a large part of what keeps him motivated.

With a quiver in his voice and through many breaks, Juan shared his story with me. One of the things he said during our interview stayed with me long after that day. He said, "If you are still a Marine, after a war, you must love what you do."

In Juan's Words

"I joined the Marine Corps right out of high school and then became a Chicago Police Officer when I was twenty-five. I had been to Desert Storm and Desert Shield, and then we got mobilized for Iraqi Freedom. My reserve unit was the Second Battalion Twenty-fourth Marines, and we went to Mahmoudiyah, Iraq. It's in the Sunni triangle also known as the Triangle of Death. Our areas of operation were Mahmoudiyah, which was our home base, Yusufiyah, which was to the west of us, and Ludafiyah to the south of us.

Our mission in Iraq was to secure the ammo and main supply roadways. The insurgents would put IEDs on the roads, so when the convoys were transporting troops or supplies or anything they would get blown up. It was our job to secure that area of operation. I was part of a team, and our job was to insert and extract the scout snipers. The snipers positioned themselves to take out the insurgents planting the bombs.

My team was a small convoy consisting of four vehicles, and because we were so small, we were often targets. I experienced several IED hits; three direct hits in a ten-day period, two back-to-back. These weren't always IED hits; sometimes it was an ambush. With the last IED, my driver was hit in the face, my gunner got hit in the back and calf, and I blew both my eardrums out and was knocked unconscious. That hit earned me a Purple Heart.

From September of 2004 to March of 2005, we had sixteen Marines killed and a lot of Marines injured in my unit. The unit before us had six killed and less injured. I had a lot of resentment toward my command and the situations they put us in, and obviously, against the enemy because ultimately that is why we were there. I have survivor's guilt and am being treated for PTSD. It's tough to call yourself a combat-injured Marine when you are standing next to a guy with amputations, so you don't say anything. When I realized that I did need help, I went in for an appointment and was asked to fill out a questionnaire. It asked questions about what I had seen and done, and I answered those. It also asked if I thought I needed help; my

104

response was yes. But I didn't receive any help. I did receive a call from the Marine Corps call center, and I indicated to them also that I needed help. There was no resolution. I ended up getting re-activated without receiving any help.

After that deployment, I ended up going back to working as a Chicago Police Officer. At the time, I didn't realize it was PTSD that was affecting my relationships not only at home but also at work. I was angry and had a lot of anxiety. In the Marines, you know what each other is going to do. We practiced it so much before going over there; there was no question about how the guy next to you would react in any situation. But being back on the police force, you know, it's a dangerous job. When I didn't feel like another officer was handling a situation correctly, I became angry. I felt my safety was at risk, but you can't talk to other cops like you talk to Marines. My wife didn't realize what was going on, and my suffering from the anxiety and getting angry caused us to fight a lot. Although I was justified in feeling the way I felt, it was my actions and my response to certain situations that were unjustified. I knew I needed help, but didn't know how bad it was.

My first son was born and shortly after that, in 2007, I was re-mobilized. It was hard to leave that time, and I was devastated. I wanted to be home with my family. Also, I had had a pretty bad falling out with my command on my previous deployment. I had felt like my command was trying to kill me; I know that sounds crazy, but I was convinced they were trying to kill me. I had also raised questions about the way we handled detainees. An Army General took over our area and corrected the way things were done, but it caused some tension between my command and I. After that, I didn't trust them, and I worried that they were going to retaliate. I fought going back, I shouldn't have even been going – I was an admin guy. The first time I asked to go but the second time they were trying to force me to go, but that wasn't my job. My job was to run service record books. In the end, I stayed and did my job at Camp Pendleton. When our unit returned from deployment, I applied to be an administrator for the Wounded Warrior Battalion at Balboa Naval Medical

Center. The intention was to help other Marines but also seek help for myself; I knew I needed it and was getting worse over time, not better.

I deactivated from my unit and went back to the police department in Chicago for a few months. I got approved to get mobilized orders to work for the Wounded Warrior Battalion. So I went back to San Diego. It was great; the Marines were all great. At that time, I felt like shit. I had a ton of problems; my anxiety was getting worse, and the PTSD was as well. Being at the Wounded Warrior Battalion gave me a second chance. I liked the command there, and they were good to me. I started to gain some self-confidence back and felt like I had an opportunity to end my career on a good note. I did well there. During that time, I would take my lunch hour to get help for myself, so I was finally in therapy. Unfortunately, I was at twenty-two years of service, and in the reserves if you don't pick up Master Sergeant by that time you are forced into retirement. My contract ended in October, but I wasn't up for promotion until the following February, so I was pushed out. I requested a medical waiver so I could stay and continue to get therapy. There was no way I could go back to the police department at that time. I knew I still needed therapy.

I had to disclose to the police department why I was going to therapy. Because of that, I was put on disability. There is too much liability for a police officer to serve with untreated PTSD. Disability pay was about half of my full pay, which I had been getting the whole time I was mobilized. So I went from two paychecks to a half of one paycheck. I couldn't afford a house and ended up sleeping in my office those last few months at Wounded Warrior Battalion. I was reserve retired with no benefits, no place to stay, broke and my wife had left me. That's when I met Sandy.

The first time I met Sandy was at the Wounded Warrior Battalion. I had extra room in my office, and one day she came in and sat at an empty desk and just started doing paperwork. I left the room and was watching her from outside a window thinking, 'Who is this lady?' I didn't say anything to her, but I didn't understand why this civilian was sitting in my office doing paperwork. She started coming in regularly, and I watched as service members and their spouses would stop by and say hello to her, stop by to give her a hug. Everyone seemed to know her name. I think she knows the name of every single service member at Balboa Naval Medical Center.

One of my Marines knew my situation, and she told Sandy about it and asked if she could help me. Sandy doesn't take no for an answer, and the Warrior Foundation stepped in and gave me a hand-up. My life had changed so drastically. I didn't know what to do; I didn't know what I was going to do or where I was going to live.

Sandy asked me to look at this place she was thinking of buying. She took me to what is now Freedom Station. They had one apartment vacant at the time. Sandy said that was where I was going to live. She doesn't take no for an answer. She paid the first month's rent and moved me in. It was nice not to be sleeping at my desk and to have at least some time to figure out what I was going to do. I didn't have any furniture or anything else. I rolled out my sleeping bag and put my clothes in little piles on the floor. I didn't need much and didn't want to ask for anything.

Every day I would go out for a run to clear my mind. One day, Sandy asked if she could bring some people by to look at the place. She was trying to get the funds to purchase the entire property and turn it into what is now Freedom Station. So Sandy came by with some people from Furnishing Hope and, while I was out on my run, they furnished the entire apartment. She put my clothes on hangers and brought gift baskets of food and toiletries. It breaks me up to think about that day, even now. It's hard to be a man and accept help. I went from being a police officer, not just any police officer; I was a Chicago Police Officer. I went from serving in the military, not just any branch of the military; I was a US Marine. To go from that to not even being able to support myself, and having strangers come in to furnish my apartment and bring me food – it was hard to accept. After going through everything I had gone through, I felt like dirt. Those times were dark times; so dark that I was hospitalized for a while. Thank God I had friends who recognized that and got me the help that I needed. Sandy made me feel like I was worthy again; she made me feel like I deserved compassion and understanding.

The uniqueness of the Warrior Foundation ~ Freedom Station is that they are hands-on. More than any other organization out there – they know the men and women they serve. They know their names, their situations, the names of their children – they care about their daily lives. I've seen other organizations; I've seen their backpacks, their t-shirts, and their commercials but have never seen them in person. That is the difference. Not to take away from the other organizations or what they might do for service members, but Warrior Foundation knows the people that they serve. They have direct contact, form direct relationships with the Marines and that's why they know their needs. Back when I first met Sandy – she was the lady that helped all the Marines. Never did I think I would end up needing her help.

I feel lucky to have watched Freedom Station form from the beginning. It looks entirely different than it did back then. After they bought the property, Sandy had all the units fixed up, converted for handicap accessibility and installed a security gate around the perimeter. It is a small community now. I've watched many people come to Freedom Station during their transition and go on to be successful people with fulfilling lives. Freedom Station gave them a place and the time they needed during the transition; a place to have time to heal.

You see a guy move in just broken. They are injured and fragile emotionally. You see them come in just messed up, and you watch the transition – they get their smile back, they get their lives back. Living in this community does something for these guys, it gives them a sense of independence, it makes them feel like other people care and they have people around them who truly understand their situation. It's hard to relate to someone who hasn't gone through what we have. I try to stay accessible to all the guys who go through Freedom Station; I can relate to them. I think it's easier for them to open up to someone who understands. Giving your time is the greatest gift you can give. I think that's what it is about the Warrior Foundation – they give you their time, their love – they don't do it for a paycheck, they do it because they sincerely care.

For me, trying to put the pieces back together is a little unique. When you get injured as an active duty guy, you get medically discharged. You still have benefits and pay. For me, getting out as a reservist, my experience is very different. It's hard going back to the civilian world after the war. I'm trying to find my passion, find out what to do from here. Being a police officer, I loved what I did; I loved my job. I was a good police officer, and I was a good Marine. Where do you go after that – nothing else compares. Finding something that you are equally passionate about when you can't be a Marine anymore, or in my case, a police officer or a Marine – it's hard. I still don't think it will ever be the same, and that's my challenge now. I'm back in school trying to gain a new skill set, and being here at Freedom Station has helped give me that time to do what I need to do to start over."

Juan is another front-man for Freedom Station. He not only helps to mentor the younger guys but also helps Sandy with fundraisers and speaking engagements. His gratitude toward Sandy and Freedom Station is apparent and rightfully so. With the support he receives and the ability to live close to the services he needs and time for school, I know he will indeed find his path and move forward while continuing to help others.

CHAPTER 18

THE VOLUNTEERS

———— ⚫ ————

Upon meeting Sandy Lehmkuhler, founder and president of Warrior Foundation ~ Freedom Station, one thing immediately stands out about her; she is passionate about helping our injured service members. Her passion isn't just something she does – it's a part of who she is. Along with an all-volunteer staff, Sandy has grown the organization into something much larger than originally intended. From its small beginning raising funds to purchase razors for the wounded at Balboa Naval Medical Center, Warrior Foundation – Freedom Station now has a transitional living facility and uses over ninety-six percent of all funds raised for assistance needed by our injured and ill service members across the nation. Although the focus is primarily the injured at Balboa, WFFS continues to lend support when needed long after the service member has moved forward, often to other states.

Sandy is fondly referred to as a surrogate or second mom by most of the warriors who have leaned on her in their time of need. She and WFFS don't disappear when the service member has made the transition back to civilian life. I have personally watched Sandy take calls from past and present warriors ranging from needing help with funeral arrangements to dog sitting. She has taught these warriors how to balance a checkbook and turn on utilities. She has helped them get into college and open a savings account. The aid that this organization offers is more than monetary; the men and women of WFFS offer their hearts.

To those who selflessly give of their time and their talents, we thank you.

Board of Directors:
Evelyn McCormick, Secretary; Judy Sexton, Director; Sandy Moul, Communications Chair; Sandy Lehmkuhler, President; Shawn Cheney, Deputy OIC, WWD NMCSD; Juliana Mercer, Chairman, Special Events; Ken Lowe, Treasurer; Jim Bedinger, Craig Blanke, Joan Mitchell, Sue Lemke, Mark Stuart, Sharron LaHaye, Rocky Sheng, Ed Hanson, Dian Self, Vic Tambone, Guy Riddle, Brian Lehmkuhler, and Mike Seymour.

Please visit www.WarriorFoundation.org to learn about Volunteer Opportunities.

CHAPTER 19

AFTER

By Ed Hanson

After my childhood
Of lilacs and wildwood
After my sign up
Marines had us line up
After the training
The sweat and the straining
After the last blast
Loss of my recent past
After the recovering
I am now discovering
After it all
Will there be love, will there be laughter
After, after it all

ACKNOWLEDGEMENT

I would like to express my heart felt thanks to the men who so openly shared their stories with me. It takes a great deal of courage to be that vulnerable.

Thank you to Warrior Foundation ~ Freedom Station board members and volunteers and special gratitude to Sandy Lehmkuhler for all you have done and continue to do for our injured service members.

To the people who make it possible for me to do what I do – thank you for seeing my craziness and loving me anyway:

Helen Gerth-Mahi, you are an amazing friend and mentor.
Toran Gaal, you own my heart. Real Forever.
Ryan, JD, Lana and Bella – I love you most!

WARRIOR FOUNDATION ~ FREEDOM STATION

Mission Statement:
Warrior Foundation ~ Freedom Station aims to be the leading force in assisting, honoring and supporting the military men and women who have so bravely served and sacrificed for our country. We are committed to helping our warriors in a variety of ways, providing quality-of-life items, numerous support services and transitional housing designed to assist them and their families during recovery.

Warrior Foundation ~ Freedom Station assists four main groups of warriors: the seriously injured just returning home from war; those suffering from post-traumatic stress or traumatic brain injury; those undergoing physical or occupational therapy, and warriors who have been medically retired and remain in our community. To serve this last group in particular, Warrior Foundation ~ Freedom Station pioneered a new approach and opened Freedom Station – a unique recovery transition center and housing facility that provides injured warriors with the acclimation time, guidance and resources to successfully make the transition from military service to civilian life.

100% of this book's profits go directly to
Warrior Foundation ~ Freedom Station

Please consider becoming a monthly or annual donor
www.WarriorFoundation.org

**WARRIOR FOUNDATION
FREEDOM STATION***

BIOGRAPHY

Greg White Jr. is a singer and songwriter from Tampa, Florida who, with his fresh, raw talent, is ready to take the world of country music by storm. His songs have been influenced by real life experiences and role models like Kenny Chesney, Alan Jackson, Blake Shelton and Garth Brooks.

His love for music began at a young age when he would fall asleep to the local country station playing softly on his clock radio. In elementary school, he wrote simple poems that later would be turned into lyrics that he would sing for his mom on the way to football practice. She would urge him to sing louder, telling him that one day he would have many people listening to his music.

"Writing songs has always come naturally," he says.

Greg now loves inspiring audiences with high-energy performances. He is already turning heads in Nashville and has had the honor of working with seasoned songwriters, including Mike Lounibos and Marty Panzer.

Ironically, it was during his two years in Japan, serving in the U.S. Navy, that Greg returned to his country roots and began performing for live audiences with *Those Rowdy Boys* – an all U.S. sailor band. This experience inspired him to take his passion to the next level and pursue music as a career. He soon learned that writing and entertaining, while his core passions, were only a part of the world of music he wanted to be immersed in. He currently attends Full Sail University working towards a Music Production degree to contribute to the industry.

Amidst a full schedule with a tour of duty in San Diego, California, several concerts and efforts to support assistance for wounded veterans, production of his first, self-titled album, Greg White Jr., is currently underway. It includes the singles "That Tree," "Long Road," and "Fullest Life," a song written as a tribute to our wounded veterans.

With his growing fan base and show schedule, Greg is reaching a market of loyal, California-based country fans.

Music is his business, his goal and his passion. He is guaranteed to energize listeners with his dynamic performances, fun-loving personality and inspirational music.

Many thanks to Greg White Jr. for creating FULLEST LIFE and for his support of veterans' organizations. Check it out on the AFTER book trailer on YouTube. Purchase Fullest Life on iTunes.

THE FULLEST LIFE

They sent me too close to hell
To fight the good fight
Now I'm here with the wounds of war
It ain't sitting right
There's a stirrin' in my spirit
A feeling in my bones
I got a chance they didn't get
I made it home

I'm gonna' get on up
I'm gonna' take a lap
I'm gonna' get my boy to his football game
We'll cheer 'em on and laugh
I'm gonna' hold the girl
That I love most in the world
I made it through the toughest fight
I'm gonna' live, gonna' live
The Fullest Life

I'm not a mountain climber
So maybe just a hike
Or I'll ride clear across
America on my bike

There's a stirrin' in my spirit
A feeling in my bones
I lift a prayer for the warriors
Who haven't made it home

I'm gonna get on up
Gonna take a lap
Gonna throw some poles in that old John boat
And hit the lake with Dad
We'll take away
Big stories from the day
And how we fought the toughest fight

I'm doing this for my brothers
Who didn't make it home

I'm gonna' get on up
Gonna share a smile
Gonna take my little girl by the hand
And walk her down the aisle
I'm lifted up
By a family built on love
I made it through the darkest night
Because they're right here by my side
N' now I'll fight the toughest fight
I'm gonna' live
Gonna' live
The Fullest Life

ABOUT THE AUTHOR

R.J. Belle began writing as a teenager as a way to express her creative side. In 2013, she found herself spending a great deal of time working on plot development and character creation, and decided to make the jump into writing for publication. After spending 15 years in the lending industry, R.J. Belle left her career to write full time and within three months, she published her first fiction mystery novel, *First One Down*.

R.J. Belle lives in Southern California with her family. She enjoys writing, reading, running, coffee, and college football. She is passionate about issues that affect our military veterans.

To see what's coming next, visit us online at
www.AuthorRJBelle.com

WE WANT TO HEAR FROM YOU!

We value feedback from our readers and are continually striving to make improvements. Please let us know how we're doing by posting an honest review on Amazon.

Made in the USA
Charleston, SC
27 April 2016